W9-BSP-203

The Great Deeds of
HEROIC WOMEN

My thanks goes to all those women who, through discussion, encouragement and practical help, have contributed to this book — especially Robin Morrow, Peg Platford, Kerry Morgan, Kath Dwyer, Veronica Green and Catherine Hammond. My special thanks goes to my wife, Norma, to whom, with Angela Ingpen, *Heroic Women* is fondly dedicated.

First American edition published by
PETER BEDRICK BOOKS
2112 Broadway
New York, NY 10023

Published by agreement with Millenium Books, Australia

Text © Maurice Saxby 1990
Illustrations © Robert Ingpen 1990
All rights reserved

Library of Congress Cataloging-in-Publication Data
Saxby, H. M. (Henry Maurice)
  The great deeds of heroic women / retold by Maurice Saxby ;
illustrated by Robert Ingpen. — 1st American ed.

  Includes bibliographical references and index.
  ISBN 0-87226-348-7
  1. Heroines – Biography. 2. Heroines in literature. 3. Women –
Legends. 4. Women – Folklore. 5. Courage. I. Title.
CT3203.S27   1991
920.72 – dc20   *91-11211*
                                                          CIP

Printed and bound in Hong Kong

10 9 8 7 6 5 4 3 2 1

98 97 96 95 94 93 92

First edition 1992

The Great Deeds of
HEROIC
WOMEN

Retold by Maurice Saxby

Illustrated by Robert Ingpen

PETER BEDRICK BOOKS
NEW YORK

CONTENTS

LIST OF ILLUSTRATIONS

The many faces of the heroic woman

"Who is this that looks forth like the dawn,
fair as the moon, bright as the sun,
terrible as an army with banners?"

The stories in this book are of extraordinary women who stir the imagination because of their courage, intelligence, boldness, forcefulness and strength of purpose. Not all are "good" women. A few are malevolent. But they all embody aspects of human nature that have existed in all societies through the ages. We all, male and female, recognise something of ourselves in these creative, fulfilled and stalwart women — or, at least, something of what we would like to be.

When I began writing the companion volume to this book, *The Great Deeds of Superheroes*, I had intended to include stories of superheroes from legend and epic; folk heroes such as Robin Hood, William Tell, Paul Bunyan and Ned Kelly; along with a sampling of heroic women. Gradually the superhero and the heroic woman took over my imagination, and it became increasingly clear that they deserved a separate volume each.

Superheroes came first, because of the obviously strong pattern of birth and behaviour that I have charted in the introductory chapter, "We all need heroes".

In the case of *Heroic Women* I could detect no such pattern. Rather, I became more and more aware of the many-faceted nature of heroic womanhood.

At first I had intended to include only women from myth and legend. But the stories of historical female heroes such as Boadicea and Joan of Arc were so potent and persistent that they demanded to be included. These are historical figures who are already part of legend. Pocahontas, too, was a legend in her own time, as was the Australian convict escapee, Mary Bryant. Their very names conjure up vivid images of determination, dignity, pride, inner strength and tragedy, for there is a tragic element in each of their stories.

The achievements of women in medicine, nursing, political science, government, the arts, sport and the humanities are now well documented. The heroic and inspiring story of the English heroine Grace Darling, for example, which captured the popular imagination in the nineteenth century, has been retold with dramatic power and psychological insight by Helen Cresswell.

The stories in this volume are of heroic women, drawn from myth and legend, history and folklore. They include goddesses, enchantresses, queens and warriors, saints and stalwart girls who are folk heroes. The latter are neither royal nor divine, but they are clever and courageous survivors.

Goddesses

The most ancient object of religious worship could well be the Great Earth Mother, the provider of food and the sustainer of life. Then came the gods, but also the goddesses, who, initially, were responsible for human sustenance.

In Greek mythology Ge (or Gaea) was the first reigning goddess, and was a divine embodiment of the earth. Her children were Uranus (Sky), Ourea (Mountains) and Pontus (Sea). Ge was infinitely wise, and was the first of the deities to prophesy through the oracle at Delphi. Zeus, who was to become the supreme ruler of the Olympian gods, was descended from Ge, as were the six chief goddesses — Hera, Athena, Artemis, Hestia, Aphrodite and Demeter. The stories of Athena, Aphrodite and Demeter are told in the opening section of this book.

Goddesses were part of the religion and worship of most cultures. Even though the Hebrew people officially worshipped only Yahweh and were forbidden to have "other gods", the Old Testament records their constant pursuit of ancient Canaanite goddesses, such as Asherah, Astarte and Anat.

Enchantresses

Less powerful than the goddesses, but potent forces in the lives and destinies of mortals, were the many enchantresses of myth and legend. Evil or malevolent women frequently possessed magical qualities, which made them forces to be feared. The stories of Circe and Medea, two of the most compelling figures in myth, are told in this book.

Along with witches and enchantresses, there existed a range of frightening female creatures, such as the three Gorgons whose faces and figures were beautiful and from whose shoulders spread glorious golden wings. But they were loathsome creatures, covered with scaly, lizard-like skin, who had hissing, writhing serpents instead of hair. They possessed boar-like tusks and their fingers were of brass. A mere glance from their eyes turned men into stone.

The multitude of hags, crones and witches of universal folklore are literary and psychological descendants of the enchantresses of the ancient world. The German Lorelei maidens and the many mermaids and sea-creatures who sing sweet, seductive songs are latter-day sirens, to be approached at the peril of a man's losing his will to theirs.

Witches belong to all cultures and story traditions, the African, American and Pacific Island societies as well as European and Asian.

Because of their literary and psychological lineage from the goddesses they have often been credited with power over the dead and have been associated with prophetic dreams, oracles and the foretelling of the future. Perhaps they represent a human longing to uncover the past and know the future.

In the Old Testament, King Saul, at a crisis point in his life, believing that he had been deserted by Yahweh, disguised himself and visited the witch of Endor by night, demanding that she conjure up for him the spirit of Samuel. When Samuel, an old man wrapped in a robe, appeared, Saul admitted his distress: "God has turned away from me and answers me no more, either by prophets or by dreams; therefore I have summoned you to tell me what I shall do."

Female warriors

The goddesses, as well as having magical powers, were sometimes involved in warfare. Ishtar was, in spite of her massive, benevolent breasts, a warrior who fought with all who tried to gain control over her.

Dilbah, the morning star in Babylonian belief, clothed herself in armour, yoked seven lions to her chariot, and set out at dawn to hunt both animals and humans.

Astarte and Anat were Canaanite goddesses of war, and Athena played a prominent role in the Trojan war.

The most famous of the ancient women warriors were the Amazons, a tribe of women who lived not far from Greece. They were ruled by two queens, one for warfare and defence and one for domestic affairs. The military queen commanded a vast array of mounted warriors who wielded double-bladed battle axes and defended themselves with ivy-shaped shields.

It has been claimed, and disputed, that each seared off her right breast so that it would not interfere with her use of the javelin or bow and arrow.

In more recent times, Boadicea epitomises the valour of the warrior queen, while Joan of Arc remains the archetypal virgin warrior.

Jewish literature has its share of strong-minded women. Although not a warrior, Judith beheaded the dreaded Holofernes without compunction. Her brave but bloody deed has inspired a multitude of paintings and is part of Jewish legend.

Saints and holy women

As well as terrorising men, the goddesses could at times inspire them, be gentle with them, and engender a nobleness of purpose. But they were seldom, except for the Chinese goddess of mercy, saintly.

Three of the five Olympian goddesses — Athena, Artemis and Hestia — were virgins, and the cult of virginity reached its height in Ancient Rome. Vesta (the Greek Hestia) was the goddess of the hearth, and her vestal virgins were priestesses who tended the fire in the temple of Vesta. Virginity has by long tradition, then, been associated with holiness, although it has never been a prerequisite for saintliness. But it is often regarded as highly desirable.

Another frequent attribute of saints is the capacity for a profound religious experience: to be able to enter a state of ecstasy and to have mystical revelations.

The Hebrew prophetesses served as a channel of communication between the human and divine worlds, but were not differentiated from their male counter-parts. So it was with the saints.

While there are both males and females in the Christian calendar of saints, intense piety and inspirational lives are universal, but "saintliness" is probably attributed more frequently to females than males. The lives of the saints, both male and female, have filled volumes.

Mortal women

In many literary traditions human beings were created by the gods, or the gods gave birth to mortals (demi-gods) who inherited something of their nature. When Zeus had a relationship with a mortal woman she gave birth to a hero.

The first mortal woman, in Greek literature, was Pandora. She was fashioned by Hephaestus, the smith and the god of fire, at the command of Zeus, who was concerned that he be worshipped by creatures who would always remain subservient to him. To prevent any threat to his power he ordered the creation of Woman, knowing that she would provide him with a powerful weapon.

When Hephaestus shaped Woman she was so beautiful that no man could resist her, but he also gave her a variety of wicked traits. She was to be called Pandora, meaning "all gifts", and she was to marry Epimetheus. Her dowry, provided by Zeus, was an ornately decorated sealed chest. Pandora was instructed that under no circumstances was she to open it.

But Zeus knew that curiosity was part of Pandora's created character. One day when she was alone, she surreptitiously eased open the lid of the box to see what was concealed inside.

It was then that all the evils that beset the world rushed out — lust, greed, pride, dishonesty, poverty, death. Swiftly Pandora snapped back the lid, but it was too late. Henceforth mortals would have to endure physical hardship, evil thoughts, emotional turmoil and spiritual anguish.

Only one attribute did Zeus allow to remain inside the box — hope. So even to this day human beings may be despairing, yet ever hopeful.

This story makes an interesting comparison with the Old Testament account of Eve's disobedience, and the eating of the fruit of knowledge.

Women in epic literature

The women behind the superheroes of ancient legend tend to remain shadowy by comparison. Mothers are often more important than wives — except for Jason, who fell in love with Medea, who not only had a will of her own, but who helped shape her husband's.

In a violent and sexist society it was the males who went adventuring and became heroes, even if they were helped in their quests by women, as Ariadne aided Theseus. Helen of Troy has gone down in literature as "the face that launched a thousand ships" over whom the Trojan war was fought. But although her name is well known and she motivated action, there are few stories about her personal exploits.

Female folk heroes

If the superwomen of epic literature are outnumbered by superheroes, there is no dearth of superheroines in folk and fairy tale. True, the Cinderellas, Snow Whites and Sleeping Beauties are more romantic and beautiful than they are daring and bold. But, as in life, there are many heroines of folk literature who qualify as superwomen either because of their intelligence and cunning or through their audacity and spirited action.

The stories told here are but a sample of the many tales of wise, courageous achievers. That many of the protagonists are both beautiful and perceptive is only appropriate. They never divest themselves of their femininity — and therein is the strength, timelessness and universality of their appeal.

Athena: Warrior Goddess of Wisdom

Athena was one of the most revered of the Immortals, the goddess of wisdom, but also the warrior goddess. Her divinity placed her above the heroes but in many ways she belonged to the heroic tradition in that she gave strength and support to the heroes, often aiding them in their exploits and offering wise advice when it was needed. Her birth, like that of many a hero, was supernatural.

Zeus, lord of Olympus, was not content with the one wife, Hera, queen of heaven. He had a roving eye and an appetite for beautiful women. For a long time he courted Metis, one of the old Titan deities, who tried to escape his suit. Once she turned herself into a fish, once into an eagle, but Zeus, too, assumed the form of a fish and then an eagle, and pursued her until she yielded to his wooing. When Metis told him that she was to bear him a child, Zeus consulted the oracle to discover whether it would be a boy or a girl. He was told by the oracle that the daughter of Metis would be surpassingly wise, talented and noble, but should Metis have a second child it would be a son who would overthrow Zeus just as Zeus had overthrown his father, Cronus.

Hera was jealous of Metis and poisoned Zeus's mind against her. One day, when Metis was taking her ease in the beautiful gardens on the shores of Lake Triton in Libya, Zeus came up behind her and swallowed her whole, as a whale gulps down a fish; partly to save her from Hera's wrath, partly so that she would not bear him a son.

Zeus was immediately aware of a violent, blinding headache that nothing could cure. In desperation he summoned Hephaestus, the crippled smith, and commanded him to cleave his skull in two and so release the evil spirit he believed was the cause of his torment. The smith-god drove a wedge into the skull of Zeus with his mighty axe, cracking it apart like the shell of a nut.

14

From the crushed cranium stepped a handsome, sturdy young woman, fully grown, gripping a spear in her right hand and steadying a shield on her left forearm. On her head shone a helmet. She wore sandals on her feet and around her breast was draped a goat-skin plate (or aegis) ornamented with a border of serpents. Her blue eyes and radiant smile won Zeus's heart. He called her "Athena Bright-Eyes" and she was at once his favourite child.

Athena was as gifted as the oracle had prophesied. Often she was asked to sit in judgement at the court of Areopagus. She was to take part in many a battle, and although she herself was never to marry she was patron to the many heroes she held dear. Her first battle was against the giants of the underworld, who attacked Zeus at a place called Phlegra in Thessaly, across the sea from Mount Olympus. In that battle Athena seemed to be in all places at once, skilfully guiding her chariot through the battlefields and engaging in hand-to-hand combat. After she killed Pallas, one of the most terrible of the giants, with her own hands, and then despatched his brother Enceladus she added Pallas to her own name and was often known as Pallas Athena.

In the Trojan War Athena fought on the side of the Greeks, and often appeared among the warriors carrying the Gorgon's head on her shield. The Greeks fashioned in her honour the gigantic wooden horse that gained them entry into the city of Troy, bringing about its downfall and ending the war.

As Odysseus journeyed home from that war, Athena was his guide, counsellor, friend and protectress, intervening to rescue him from many a difficulty. For she was not a goddess of violence so much as a deity who inspired courage and who guided by wise reason and enlightenment. She was a friend and guide to Perseus, Achilles and other heroes, and she assisted Argus the master shipwright when he was commissioned by Jason to build the *Argo*. When that task was completed Athena tied a magic oak branch to the prow — a branch that could on occasion foretell the future and proffer advice to those who sailed in the *Argo*.

Through a more peaceful contest, and again because of her wisdom, she became the patron goddess of Athens, where she is still honoured today. Athenians love to tell the story of the quarrel between Athena and Poseidon as to who should be granted the patronage of that city. The gods were called to arbitrate and they decreed that the contest should be decided in favour of whoever should provide the city with the finest gift.

Poseidon, god of the sea, struck a rock with his trident, and from it gushed a salt spring. But Athena butted her spear against the ground, from whence sprang an olive tree, its grey-green leaves promising shade, its dark ripe fruit providing both food and oil — oil for their cooking, their lamps and for anointing their bodies. Athena was proclaimed the winner of the contest and her gift can be seen today growing by the Acropolis.

This was but one of her gifts to humanity. She it was who showed men how to make the wheel, the axe and the plough. She inspired them to make sails for their ships; she taught them to make music upon the flute and the trumpet.

It was Athena who was the first to spin wool and she taught women the arts of spinning, weaving and household crafts. But she was first and always an Immortal, and like her fellow deities she was intolerant of any mortal who challenged the power and position of the gods. Such arrogance was called *hubris* by the Greeks, and was always followed by *nemesis* or retribution. How Athena brought nemesis to Arachne is one of the most famous stories connected with the goddess.

Athena and Arachne

Arachne was a country girl, the daughter of Idmon of Colophon in Lydia, a country famous for its spinning and weaving and for a purple dye with which artisans coloured their cloth. Arachne was famous throughout the land for her weaving. When she wove a huge tapestry depicting in fine detail many of the exploits of the gods, the boast went up in Lydia that the girl was indeed the finest weaver in the world. The girl herself boasted that her fingers could fly faster than those of her rivals, that her patterns were more intricate and evenly worked than those of Athena herself. So arrogant did she become that news of her boasting reached the goddess, who at first was curious but then became angry. Athena decided to visit the girl and see for herself what marvels she wove into her tapestries, and if necessary draw her into a contest.

Disguised as a withered old woman, Athena visited the girl at her loom. Looking at a picture of Poseidon dashing through the waves in his chariot, the goddess murmured, "You have done well, my girl. Almost as well as I could do, when I was your age and my fingers were swift and supple."

"Never," replied the girl. "No one is, or has been, my equal. My tapestries are the finest, most detailed and most intricate in the world."

"Is that so! What of the goddess Athena?" queried the crone. "I hear tell that she is the finest craftswoman in the world."

"Not so. Once, maybe, I could have learned a stitch or two from her, but not now. My skill is unparalleled and unsurpassed. Not even Athena can match me!" And Arachne tossed her head defiantly.

The old woman's eyes hardened, and she drew her lips into a thin line of disapproval. "Arrogant words, my dear. Perhaps you would care to make good your boast?"

So saying, Athena dropped her disguise and the Immortal stood before the girl, her face flushed with anger.

16

"Set up a loom for me," she ordered the nymphs who were watching the encounter. Then she turned to Arachne. "Your idle boasting has troubled my ears. Those who defy the gods must make good their words. Now let us weave side by side and we shall see who weaves a finer tapestry!"

News of the contest spread quickly. Shepherds came from their fields, nymphs stole from the glades to watch.

Athena worked confidently at her loom, never glancing at Arachne, who toiled beside her. A bright tapestry formed under the flying fingers of the patron of the crafts. With her shuttle she painted a picture of Nemesis, the goddess of vengeance, bearing away one who dared challenge the Immortals. Arachne too, worked swiftly and surely. With her shuttle she wove pictures of the gods caught in acts of foolishness and indiscretion.

Each of the contestants chose their colours unerringly, each wove with precision and deftness. The pictures glowed with life.

When the tapestries were finished, each looked in judgement at the work of the other. As Athena examined Arachne's tapestry the girl held her head high in defiance. But when the goddess saw what the girl had done, Arachne's impertinence drove her to blazing anger.

Her furious hands tore at the tapestry. With her shuttle as a weapon she hacked at it and tore it apart. Then she turned on the girl herself and struck at her with her self-made weapon.

Ashamed and frightened, pale and distraught, Arachne turned away from the horrified gaze of the surrounding nymphs and shepherds. She stumbled into the woods close by and, unloosing her girdle, she hanged herself from a tree — a wan, pathetic, tattered remnant of a once-proud mortal.

Athena followed her into the forest, and when she saw the sad evidence of her wrath her heart softened, and she leaned forward and touched the figure hanging by the flimsiest of girdles: "Continue to weave, poor lass, but weave to sustain your life. Each thread that you weave will be the finest that earth has known, each web the most delicate and intricate. Only when the dew sparkles in its tracery will it be noticed. Only then will people compare your work with that of the Immortals."

Even as Athena spoke Arachne's body shrivelled and her girdle shrank to a single thread. A tiny spider hung suspended, then slowly it began to spin its thread of silk. Then it wove its web. When night fell the dew formed, and as the sun rose Arachne looked on her work and knew that it was the finest the world had known.

Athena never married, and she bore no children. But her spirit lives on, not only in Greece, but wherever women help temper aggression with wisdom and understanding, which is the way of heroes.

Aphrodite: Goddess of Love

The Greek goddess of love was known to the Romans as Venus. Botticelli's famous painting, *The Birth of Venus*, which hangs in the Ufizzi gallery in Florence, shows the goddess rising from the sea-foam from whence, according to Hesiod, the eighth-century Greek poet, she was born. Homer, however, makes her the daughter of Zeus and Diana and therefore one of the gods and goddesses of Mount Olympus. She could well be a Greek version of the Asian goddess, Astarte. In Greece she was worshipped in two different manifestations: Aphrodite Uranos — a high, celestial, pure form of love, and Aphrodite Pandemos — physical, sensual love.

She was particularly honoured at Cyprus, thought by many to be her birthplace. She was the patroness of sailors because of her birth, and also the goddess of beauty and marriage. Strangely, in Sparta she was looked upon as a war goddess. Because Paris awarded her the apple of beauty in his now-famous judgement, she supported the Trojans in their war against the Greeks, and on one occasion she went to battle in order to rescue Paris when he was in danger.

Statues show the goddess either naked or as a draped figure holding her favourite bird, a dove, in her hands. Her handmaidens, the Graces and the Horae, often stood around to serve her. Poets sang of her beauty and men everywhere succumbed to her charms.

It was off the coast of Cythera, where, according to legend, the sea-foam gathered itself together and gave birth to the maiden, conceived when the sea was impregnated with the blood and the life-force of the sky god, Uranus. She rose, fully formed and beautiful beyond measure, from the arms of the sea. A gentle zephyr, born of Zephyrus, god of the west wind, took the lovely creature in his arms and bore her shoreward. As she stepped onto the earth grass grew beneath her feet and flowers sprang up, already blooming, from the ground on which she walked.

Standing at the sea's verge, the maiden lifted her arms to wring the salt water from her long, gold-red hair. As she did so, three sprightly and comely daughters of Zeus, the Graces, appeared before her and attended to her person, garlanded her with roses and clothed her in a flowing robe.

As they stood there, a conch shell floated into sight on the sea, and was carried by a wave to the shore. As the beauteous maiden stepped into it, the zephyr blew the raft-shell softly into the tide that was to carry it serenely to the island of Cyprus.

On the island, attendants waited to escort the new goddess, to join Zeus, along with her brothers and sisters, on Mount Olympus.

In due course Aphrodite, who turned the head of every man who looked upon her beauty, was married to the god of the forge, Hephaestus, to whom she bore a daughter, Harmonia. In the years to come Harmonia was to marry Cadmus, who founded the Grecian city of Thebes.

Although Aphrodite was possessed of great physical grace and beauty and was attended by the three Graces and the Horae — the goddesses of the seasons — she could not always control the turbulence of the sea, which ran deep in her veins. Nothing pleased her more than to meddle in the lives of mortals, bringing confusion, and sometimes tragedy, into their lives. No matter what pain she caused her victims, the goddess remained indifferent to their sufferings. She had no more care for the gods themselves, and was repeatedly unfaithful to her husband. She took not only Ares, the god of war, as a lover, but many mortals also.

It was an incredibly beautiful youth, Adonis, who stirred such a passion in the goddess that the story of her love for Adonis became known throughout the ancient world.

The story begins with the mother of Adonis. Her name was Myrrha, sometimes known as Smyrna, who was the daughter of Theias, the King of Syria. Myrrha was a girl with a mind of her own. Because she refused to give Aphrodite due honour, the goddess cursed her and made her fall in love with her own father. To protect Myrrha from her father's wrath and to prevent him from killing her, the gods mercifully turned the girl into a tree, the myrrh-tree.

Ten months later the bark of the tree peeled away, and the tree gave birth to Adonis. Aphrodite was so moved by the beauty of this child that she gave him to Persephone, queen of Hades, to raise in her domain under the earth.

Persephone herself was smitten with the beauty of Adonis, and when Aphrodite demanded him for herself a great quarrel broke out. So bitter was the antagonism between the two goddesses that Zeus stepped in and decreed that Adonis should spend a third of the year with Aphrodite, a third with Persephone and the other third with which ever one he pleased. Adonis chose to spend one-

third of the year in the underworld. The rest of the year he would live and hunt in the world above.

As the years went by, Adonis grew in beauty and became a mighty hunter, with Aphrodite frequently by his side. But Ares, who was still infatuated by Aphrodite, was jealous of the youth. It was probably Ares who sent the wild boar that, in spite of Aphrodite's frequent warnings to Adonis to be careful, gored the youth in the thigh one day while he was out hunting. Adonis was mortally wounded.

Aphrodite hastened to be with her beloved, this most handsome of men, now with his life's blood ebbing away. As she sped through the forest she had to force her way through a thicket, sharp with thorns. One of the thorns, longer and sharper than the rest, pierced her foot, and drew blood. The rose of the thicket, that until then had been white, now turned to crimson, and has remained so to this day. From the trail of blood left by Adonis, which was watered with the tears of Aphrodite, there sprang up anemones, which even now flower in spring in the lands of the eastern Mediterranean.

To honour Adonis, Aphrodite inspired worshippers, who praised him as a god of the returning summer season. In Syria, women planted seeds in shallow soil and in vases each spring, then watered them with warm water. It is said that these plants sprouted immediately but withered at once, and they were known as "gardens of Adonis".

Although Aphrodite mourned the death of Adonis, she remained restless and impetuous. She was not beyond throwing taunts at others of the Immortals who had had affairs with mortals, especially those gods who had fathered children in the world beyond Olympus. In spite of her great love for Adonis, never had she had a child by him, she reminded those who dared to answer her back.

Aphrodite became known as a trouble-maker to the dwellers of Olympus, who so complained of her to Zeus that he at last decided to put a stop to her taunts. He would beat Aphrodite at her own game.

There was, at that time, a Trojan prince named Anchises who tended his father's flocks on the slopes of Mount Ida. Anchises, like Adonis, was beautifully formed, strong, supple of limb and strikingly handsome.

One day, as Aphrodite passed by Mount Ida in her swan-drawn chariot, Zeus willed her to look down to where Anchises was herding his sheep. As Aphrodite's gaze fell on the young man, Eros, the god of love, loosed an arrow (by Zeus's command), which lodged itself in Aphrodite's heart. A dart from the bow of Eros always worked instantly. Aphrodite was at once smitten with a love for Anchises that was more passionate even than her infatuation with Adonis.

But although Aphrodite was impetuous, she could also be cautious. Mortal men were loath to have romantic dealings with Immortals — the odds against them were too great, and seldom did any good come of such affairs.

So Aphrodite restrained herself for the moment, and planned how best she could win the love of this young man. She would disguise herself as a mortal, a princess, and appear before Anchises, who would find her irresistible; for what man could fail to respond when the goddess of love, in whatever form, stood before him?

Nevertheless, Aphrodite prepared herself with care, even dispensing with her girdle, symbol of her divinity. Her beauty would win him, and her charm.

Clothed in the garments of royalty, Aphrodite sped once again to Mount Ida in her chariot. Dismissing the Graces who still attended her, she made her way to where Anchises had pitched his tent. The prince was plucking at the strings of his lyre when Aphrodite appeared before him. There was no need of an arrow from Eros. Aphrodite's presence commanded the love of any mortal man who beheld her beauty.

"Who are you? From whence do you come?" were the words Anchises spoke. "How beautiful you are, my love, how beautiful you are!" sang his heart.

"I hear my beloved. See how he has come leaping from the mountains like a young stag. The season of glad songs has come. Come then, my love, my lovely one, come..." So responded the heart of Aphrodite.

But with her lips she lied, saying, "I am the daughter of the King of Phrygia and I need your protection, for a great ill has befallen me."

"Fear not. With my life I will protect you, for I too am royal, a prince of Troy. Tell me your story."

With honeyed words Aphrodite told her prepared story, of how she had been carried off by Hermes, the messenger of the gods, who had abducted her to this mountainside to become the bride of a shepherd-prince. As she gazed on Anchises her eyes told him all that he needed to know.

"How beautiful are your feet, your eyes, your hair, your body, O royal daughter. I feel swamped with a love that no flood can quench, no torrent drown." So sang the mind of Anchises.

Then he held the goddess in his arms and declared his love. And she assented to all he asked of her, and the couple lived together as man and wife. Only then did Aphrodite reveal her true identity to her husband.

"Promise me, my love, that you will tell no one my secret. Humans are wary of the gods, for we breathe a different air, but I promise you that I will bear you a son of whom you will be proud, and whose name will go down in history."

The son whom Aphrodite gave to Anchises was Aeneas, who was to become the father of the Roman people, after the fall of Troy.

Anchises for a long time nursed Aphrodite's secret in his heart, and said nothing. But one feast-day, after he had drunk freely of the new wine, his tongue was loosened, and he began to brag that he was married to no ordinary woman, but to the goddess Aphrodite herself.

This was the end of Aphrodite's passionate love for Anchises. She must go her way, and he his. But it was not quite so simple. In boasting of his relationship with Olympus, Anchises had aroused the anger of Zeus. Some say that Zeus punished the mortal by making him blind. But others say that Zeus, in his anger, hurled a thunder-bolt at Anchises, which hit him in the thigh and crippled him. Years later, when Troy was sacked by the Greeks, it was Aeneas who, given divine help by Aphrodite, hoisted his handicapped father onto his shoulders and carried him from the doomed city. From there, father and son escaped to Sicily, where Anchises died and was buried, while Aeneas wandered for many years until he came to the Kingdom of Latium, near the future site of Rome. His story is told in the *Aeneid*, a long poem in Latin, by the poet Virgil.

Many are the stories told about Aphrodite, not a few of them scandalous. When she became the lover of Ares, the god of war, who himself was notoriously profligate, Helios the sun god made it his business to gossip to Hephaestus, Aphrodite's true husband. Hephaestus, the smith, became so enraged that he forged a large, strong but invisible net in which he one day trapped Aphrodite and Ares while they were together, and paraded them in humiliation, before the other gods and goddesses on Olympus.

When she loved, Aphrodite loved passionately, and she would fight savagely to protect those whom she loved. She hated just as fiercely as she loved, and her rages and curses were greatly feared. When the women of Lemnos refused to worship her, she sent a horrendous odour upon their land to plague them. When she was offended by King Cinyras of Paphos, she forced his daughters to give themselves to strangers.

She is perhaps best remembered for her involvement in the Trojan war. Aphrodite was one of three goddesses on Mount Olympus who claimed the apple thrown by Eris, known also as Discord, into the banquet hall on Olympus, marked "For the Fairest of All". Paris, the son of Priam of Troy, who, like Anchises, watched his father's flocks on Mount Ida, was appointed the judge in the dispute.

Each of the three goddesses tried to buy Paris's favour. Hera offered to make him lord of Europe and Asia; Athena to make him invincible in war; but Aphrodite offered him the hand of the most beautiful woman in the world, Helen. When Paris awarded Aphrodite the apple she honoured her bargain, but when Paris carried Helen away to Troy the Greeks laid siege to the city, and the Trojan war had begun.

Throughout the siege of Troy, Aphrodite gave Paris her protection. It was she who kept him safe in his duel with Menelaus, the husband of Helen. To the Trojans, Aphrodite, with all her faults, was both a goddess and heroine whom they could admire, but their admiration would always be tinged with respect, even fear. And this is how people regard Aphrodite, even today.

Demeter: Goddess of the Grain

Demeter was the Greek goddess of the harvest, the earth and its fertility. She was also known to the Greeks as Deo; and the Romans called her Ceres. She was the daughter of Cronus and Rhea and joined her brothers and sisters on Mount Olympus. Beloved of Zeus, she bore him a daughter, Persephone, while to the mortal, Iasion, she bore Plutus, the god of wealth and of the earth. Demeter's true concerns were not on Olympus, but on the earth, where she presided over the fertility of the crops, grain in particular. She is best remembered for her love of her beautiful daughter, Persephone. Because similar stories are told about the Egyptian goddess Isis, the Greeks often identified the two goddesses.

Demeter and her daughter Persephone lived on the mountainous island of Sicily. Persephone grew to womanhood in peaceful rural surroundings, far from the quarrels and rivalries of the Immortals on Mount Olympus. Each year Demeter ripened the grain to gold, and at the end of each summer harvest the people gathered to give thanks for her goodness and bounty. Persephone, the Flower Maiden, was one of the loveliest and most beautiful girls in Ancient Greece. She grew up carefree and strong, a companion of nymphs, fleet of foot and pleasing to the eyes of all men.

Deep in the underworld, Hades, Persephone's uncle, ruled as King. He was lonely, and dissatisfied with his dark, dreary existence. When he saw the fresh beauty of Persephone as she walked through the fields above, he begged Zeus to give him the Flower Maiden to be his wife. Zeus, who knew that Demeter would never consent to such a match, told Hades that if he wanted the maiden he would have to snatch her away secretly in Demeter's absence.

25

One golden day that same year, Persephone and her companions were in a secluded valley gathering wildflowers. They darted joyfully from clumps of violets to stands of iris and hyacinth. Persephone, running ahead of her friends, spied a flower whose fragile beauty drew her further into the valley. The flower was heavily perfumed, and from around its base sprang a multitude of sweet-smelling blooms. It was a flower planted by Hades himself — the flower of death.

As Persephone stretched gracefully forward to pluck the main stem, the earth at her feet was split assunder, and out through the gaping crevasse appeared dark Hades in his ebony chariot drawn by gleaming black horses.

Like an engulfing shadow the black king of the underworld seized the terrified girl and carried her down to his kingdom so swiftly that only Hecate, the queen of black magic and evil ghosts, saw her go.

When night fell and Perspehone failed to return home, her mother sent out a search-party; and Demeter joined the searchers, lighting torches from the fires of the volcano, Etna, so as to search through nine long, grief-filled days and nights. She ate no food, she didn't wash, and she took no rest. On the tenth night, when no moon shone, Hecate came out of her cave and appeared before the bereft mother.

"Hail Demeter, controller of the seasons and queen of the harvest. I know not who has stolen your daughter, but stolen she was, for with my own eyes I saw her snatched from the land and carried away in a great black chariot; but the head of the charioteer was shrouded in darkness and I know not his name."

Thanking the queen of the night, Demeter continued her search throughout the days and at night with a torch held in each hand. At last she approached Helios, the sun-god, the eye of the world, catching him as he drove the chariot of the sun down into the western ocean to be ferried across it ready for the eastern sunrise. Helios, who looked down upon gods and men alike, was wise in the ways of mortals and immortals, and was both fair and just.

To Demeter's pleadings he made answer: "Mighty Zeus himself is the one to blame for your loss. He it must have been who gave your daughter to Hades. And remember, Demeter — Hades, too, is a god and brother to Zeus, so is no unfit husband for your daughter, Persephone."

But Demeter refused to be comforted and blazed with anger. Disguising herself as a mortal woman, she wandered from land to land, and so obsessed was she with her quest that she forgot the needs of the mortals whom she served. Plants and trees died because of her neglect, the grain harvest failed and the land withered into barrenness.

At last, in the guise of an old woman, she came to Eleusis, where she sat on a stone, which from that time has been known as "the stone without joy". From there she made her way to the palace of the king, where she was received kindly by the king's daughters. They led her into the house and introduced the goddess to their mother, the queen Metaneira, who, not recognising Demeter as one of the Immortals, took her into the household to be a nurse to her infant son, Demophoön.

Some nights later Queen Metaneira stumbled upon a strange sight. Demophoön's nursemaid was holding the child by one leg and dangling him over the kitchen fire. Metaneira's terrified scream startled Demeter who dropped the infant, unharmed but whimpering.

Confronted by the angry queen, Demeter was forced to reveal her true identity. She explained to the astonished mother that each day she had anointed the infant with ambrosia, the nectar of the gods, then held him over the sacred flames in order to make the boy immortal by burning away his mortal elements.

Wearily Demeter told the queen that by interfering she had lost the gift of immortality for her son. The goddess, still sore at heart, then set out once again in search of her daughter.

A whole year passed. No crops were gathered and the granaries of the ancient world were sadly depleted. The world order was in chaos. Zeus, looking down from Mount Olympus, determined that something must be done to restore harmony to the saddened earth.

So he summoned Iris, a golden-winged messenger and goddess of the rainbow, to implore Demeter to have pity on the troubled world and to spread her bounty once more across the earth.

"Not until Zeus commands Hades to restore my daughter to the land of the living," the goddess responded. "Until then the earth shall be as barren as the driest desert." And she remained deaf to all entreaties.

At last Zeus sent Hermes, his son and messenger, to Hades deep in his nether-kingdom, seated on his gloomy throne with his pale-faced, weary-eyed bride at his side. Dead, dried flowers drooped from her hands and every so often she distractedly pulled one from the bunch and let it fall to the ground.

Hermes stood before the dark king. "Zeus, our father, bids me return Persephone to the land above, or else Demeter has sworn to blot out the race of man. Should that happen, your kingdom will eventually be no more. Release her, provided no food has passed her lips while she has dwelt in the kingdom of the dead."

"Go then," said Hades to Persephone. "Zeus has commanded it. But do not feel anger toward me, for I am truly worthy to be your husband, and while you are with me you are queen of all who dwell below."

As Persephone rose through the chasm of the underworld and stepped from Hermes' chariot it was as though the world was born anew. Spring had come in an instant. From the newly moist earth sprang green shoots of grain, and almond trees burst into blossom.

But deep in the underworld Hades was questioning his subjects. When he came to Ascalaphus, a son of the nymph of the Styx and who dwelt by Acheron, the second river of the dead, Ascalaphus, the informer, spoke up: "I saw Persephone while she was walking in the garden of Hades take a pomegranate to quench her thirst, and I swear by the river Styx that she swallowed three of its seeds."

Zeus, when told of this, summoned Hades, Demeter and Persephone before him.

"It is true," said Persephone, "three seeds did I swallow."

In anger Demeter turned on Ascalaphus and had him imprisoned beneath a great stone in Hades as a warning to all informers. And later she turned him into an owl, a bird of ill omen who prophesies misfortunes to come as it flies through the night. Turning to Zeus she declared that if her daughter were forced to return to Hades, she would once again bring desolation to the soil and cause death to all green and growing things.

A furious discussion broke out among the gods, until Zeus made a solemn declaration. For nine months of the year Persephone could dwell on earth with her mother, but for the remaining three she must return to Hades as queen of the dead.

"So be it," said Demeter. But from that year onward, when Persephone descended to her husband's realm Demeter put on mourning and the earth mourned with her. The flowers faded and died, the trees shed their leaves and the soil lay cold and bare. Even the song of the birds was stilled. But each year as Persephone ascended through the crevasse from the underworld, spring arrived. Flowers sprang up beneath her feet, trees and vines burst into bud and blossom and began to fruit, the olives turned softly green as birds burst into song, calling to one another across blue skies.

So it was then and is to this day.

Atalanta: The Fleet-footed Huntress

Even though the female gods of Ancient Greece were for the most part a strong-minded, spirited lot and there was no shortage of quick-witted, able princesses and noblewomen, the role of hero was almost exclusively male. The daughters of the gods and high-born females were usually both beautiful and clever — sometimes to the point of craftiness and cunning — and destined to be wives or mothers of heroes. While they sometimes set tasks or were the cause of heroic trials and encounters, they were physically more passive and less adventurous than their male counterparts. Like Penelope they tended to remain at home faced with their own trials and tribulations while their husbands journeyed forth and participated in feats of strength, endurance, physical prowess and skill.

An exception was Atalanta, but even she was outwitted by a man — or so the story goes.

Atalanta was a princess of Arcadia, the daughter of King Iasus of Tegea, who, because he was thwarted in his wish for a son, left her as a baby to die on a harsh mountain slope. She was found by a she-bear, who suckled her and brought her up as one of her cubs, until the girl was discovered by hunters who reared her as one of their own kind. Consequently she grew up fleet of foot, strong and physically able. Once when she was attacked by two centaurs, she shot them both dead with her arrows, for she was a splendid huntress, having been trained by the immortal huntress, Artemis, who regarded her as one of her nymphs.

Not only was Atalanta fleet-footed but she was free-spirited also, her own person. When the oracle declared that should she marry she would one day be changed into an animal, she took her place with the youthful heroes but allowed her heart to feel fondness for none of them. Proudly she refused all offers of love and marriage.

One of her suitors was Meleager, who had sailed with Jason as one of the Argonauts and who had fallen in love with Atalanta during the voyage of the *Argo* — she was the only woman to be allowed to take part in the expedition.

When Meleager returned to Calydon after the quest for the Golden Fleece he found the inhabitants terrorised by a ferocious wild boar, which was laying waste the crops and killing anyone who attempted to hunt it down.

So Meleager organised a great hunt. He called together a large gathering of heroes who had sailed on the *Argo* including Heracles, Theseus and Jason himself. He sent a special invitation to Atalanta because of her skill as a huntress and because he wanted to marry her. Although the heroes welcomed her, the presence of a woman aroused both scorn and anger among some of the hunting party, especially Meleager's uncles, Phexippus and Toxeus, who were brothers of his mother, Queen Althaea.

"Who are we, to hunt with a maiden! Let her remain at her loom, which is more fitting for a woman!" they protested, forgetting that Artemis, goddess of the hunt, had herself taught Atalanta the skills of hunting.

Meleager would have none of their petty complaints. He and Atalanta stalked together, the girl holding her long bow gracefully in the left hand, her quiver full of sharp-tipped arrows around her neck, her long hair held back with a garland and flowing in tresses over her shoulder.

Through forest glades to a rushy marsh the party travelled, and there the great boar, with tusks like sharpened daggers, was flushed from its lair. The hearts of even these mighty heroes quailed. One by one the hunters loosed their arrows and missed.

Then Atalanta held the boar in position with her eye. She fitted an arrow to her bow, which she held taut. With a prayer to Artemis, she fired, and the arrow sped swift and straight. It pierced the head of the boar just above the right ear. Even so, the tough skin held the arrow fast so that it stopped short of the brain.

The maddened creature thrashed the undergrowth and charged violently in every direction. One hunter who tried to finish it off with an axe was himself gored to death; another was impaled on his own spear, so wild was the confusion. Even Theseus's aim faltered and his spear flew wide. Only Meleager stayed cool, and it was his arrow that finished the work that Atalanta's had begun.

Amid the shouts and cheers of the hunters and heroes Meleager crouched and skinned the boar, holding out its head and hide to Atalanta saying "Lady, we share the spoils as we share the honour, for your arrow was the first to strike; mine only followed!"

Meleager's uncles were enraged. This, they felt, was adding insult to insult. Their resentment boiled over and they snatched away the skin, shouting insults at the maiden who, for Meleager's sake, looked them coldly in the eye but did nothing to avenge herself.

But Meleager's anger could not be contained, and it erupted like lava from a volcano. With a curse he drew his sword, stabbing Phexippus first and then sending Toxeus to join him in his death throes. Returning the head and hide of the boar to the huntress, he gathered the party together and they returned to Calydon carrying the bodies of the dead hunters and Meleager's two uncles.

Queen Althaea was waiting. The news of her brothers' deaths preceded the party and she beat her fists with grief and rage. Her mind clouded, and she rushed to her chamber, where she had hidden in a chest the remnants of a charred, burnt firebrand — a piece of wood that had been burning in her room seven days after the birth of Meleager. On that day she had been visited by the three daughters of Zeus known as the three Fates. On that same day one of the grim sisters had foretold that Meleager's life would end as soon as the log that was burning in her room was reduced to ashes. When she heard this awful pronouncement Althaea snatched the brand from the hearth and placed it in the chest, where it had remained all these years. Now she took it from its hiding place and flung it into the fire, where it quickly caught alight, flared and was consumed to ashes.

Meleager was already celebrating the death of the boar, the return of the hunting party and especially the skill of Atalanta, to whom he now raised his glass. Even as he turned to drink, the glass crashed to the floor, and the hero who held it felt a searing pain, fell into a swoon and died.

The queen, who had rushed to the banqueting room and saw what she had done, hanged herself, so that the celebration turned to mourning — on two accounts. The Calydonian boar hunt had ended in tragedy.

Atalanta's Race

After the hunting of the Calydonian boar and the death of Meleager, Atalanta was acknowledged by her father, King Iasus. So she went to live at his court in Tegea at Arcadia.

It was her father's wish that she marry so that she and her husband could succeed him on the throne. Atalanta still remembered the prophecy of the oracle, and was determined not to marry. To overcome her father's pleas she formed a plan.

"I will only marry," she announced, "the one who can out-run me in a race. Let any suitor challenge me. The first to beat me shall marry me, but whoever loses will forfeit his life!"

So famous had she become, not only for her beauty and swift-footedness but also because of her hunting of the great boar, that suitors came from near and far to challenge the princess even though they knew the consequences would be fatal

if they lost. For time and again Atalanta would allow her challenger a slight lead; then she would pursue him with a lance in her hand, dealing him a mortal blow as she caught up with him. The head of the loser would be placed on the finishing-post of the now infamous racetrack. Gradually the rush of suitors became a trickle and then ceased, as princes throughout the known world perished in their attempt to win Atalanta's hand.

Then her cousin, Prince Melanion, came to visit and straightaway fell in love with her proud bearing, her long, lean limbs and her smouldering beauty. But the prince knew that he was no match for the huntress in a footrace. So he took himself to the Temple of Aphrodite, the goddess of love and beauty, where he prayed and made offerings to the immortal queen. Aphrodite was displeased with Atalanta for defying her for so many years, and was all too ready to help Melanion. Sheathed in a veil of glory, she appeared by his side and slipped into his hand three golden apples plucked from the Garden of the Hesperides by Athena herself. Then Aphrodite whispered words of counsel into the ear of the prince.

Melanion presented himself formally at the court of Iasus and entered his name as challenger in a race with Atalanta.

Crowds lined the racetrack. The couple took their places, the signal was given and the race began. So swift of foot were both contestants that they sped over the track without leaving a single footprint. But Atalanta enjoyed playing games with her suitors. For a time she allowed Melanion to draw ahead, but the prince had been well briefed by Aphrodite. As he felt her breath on his shoulder he rolled one of the golden apples into her path.

The maiden's eyes gleamed as she was filled with the desire to possess the golden fruit. She faltered for a moment, stooped and gathered it up, but in doing so she fell behind in the race.

Again she drew close to her rival, and was about to overtake him when he rolled a second apple into her path. Once more she hesitated, and once again, overcome by her desire, she stooped and gathered it up. Again she had fallen behind.

Now the finishing post was in sight. Neck and neck like two racing horses, the couple sped along the track. For a third time Atalanta allowed herself to drop back. For a third time Melanion heard the swish of her sandals and felt the rush of her breath. For a third time he dropped the fascinating fruit in her way. For an instant the girl knew that she was being tricked, but even as the certainty came to her she paused to scoop up the apple of the sun.

As she straightened up and prepared for a final burst of speed a roar went up from the onlookers. Melanion had reached the finishing-line ahead of her and won the race. But not only the race, he had also won her heart. For does not Aphrodite rule the hearts of both men and women, even to the point of their tempting fate?

So Melanion and Atalanta were wed and became king and queen of Tegea, and a son was born who was to rule in their place.

But the oracle had spoken truly. One day when Melanion and Atalanta were in the woods hunting they sheltered in a temple dedicated to Zeus and made love there. The lord of Olympus was outraged by their behaviour and turned them into lions, and the prophecy was fulfilled.

Circe:
The Enchantress

Circe was the daughter of Helios, the Greek sun-god, and the sea-nymph, Perse, a daughter of Oceanus. She was sister to Aeëtes, King of Colchis, and lived alone with her servants on the island of Aeaea, said to be off the west coast of Italy. She had come there from Colchis in her father's chariot.

Sometimes she was regarded as a goddess, at times a nymph. But always she is a figure who takes a strong hold on the imagination, for she is renowned for her pastime of turning any travellers who visited her palace into animals.

When Circe first beheld Picus, the son of Saturn, she fell immediately and violently in love with him. When, however, she let Picus see how she felt, he was revolted and spurned her advances. Besides, he was in love and betrothed to the nymph, Canens. Circe, in spite, turned Picus into a woodpecker.

Soon Circe achieved the reputation of being an amorous young witch. Another of her victims was Glaucus, the sea god, who visited Circe begging her for a love potion to give to Scylla, the daughter of Phorkys and Hecate. Circe looked lovingly on Glaucus and wanted him for herself, but he was so much in love with Scylla that he had eyes for no one but her. The sorceress became violently angry, but knew that her magic could not be used against a god, so she gave Glaucus a potion, pretending that it would fill Scylla with love for him. Instead, it turned Scylla into a hideous, six-headed sea-monster who was to lurk in the Straits of Messina, between Sicily and Italy. Whenever a ship passed her way, she would seize six of the crew, and devour them.

Circe was known through the ancient world because of her magical powers. Jason was one of the first to consult her.

When Jason, the Argonaut, fled from Colchis with the golden fleece, accompanied by Medea, who was also a sorceress, they were pursued by Apsyrtus, Medea's brother. Offshore from an island sacred to Artemis, Jason and

Apsyrtus held a parley. Apsyrtus agreed to allow Jason to retain the golden fleece, provided he left Medea behind on the sacred island.

Medea, however, taunted Jason with not really loving her then treacherously promised to lure her brother into Jason's hands. If Jason wouldn't kill Apsyrtus himself, she would. Jason was stung into action.

So when Medea tricked Apsyrtus into landing alone on the island by pretending that Jason had kidnapped her, Jason slew the defenceless youth. The bloodiest account of this story says that Jason cut off the fingers and toes from Apsyrtus' corpse, then three times ritually sucked up and spat out his blood in an attempt to atone for his treachery.

Zeus was outraged by his behaviour, however, and swore that the Argonauts would never reach their home again unless they were purified of this heinous crime.

So Jason and Medea sought out Circe, whom they found waiting for them on the shore of her island home.

Silently Jason and Medea followed the sorceress to her house. There she performed a ritual with the blood of a pig and offered sacrifices to Zeus. It was not until the ritual was complete that Circe asked the couple who they were. Medea, speaking in the language of the Colchians, told Circe, who was also her aunt, all about how she helped Jason, but left out the fact that Jason had murdered her brother. Shocked by Medea's account of her conduct toward her father, Circe ordered Medea to leave; but as Zeus had accepted the sacrifices offered on their behalf, the couple had already been purified. So they were able to continue their journey, cleansed.

Many years later, Odysseus arrived at the island of Aeaea in his last remaining ship. Before exploring the island Odysseus divided his men into two groups and then drew lots to see which one would reconnoitre. It fell to Odysseus to stay and guard the camp and to his cousin, Eurylochus, and his men to go exploring.

At the end of a long day of waiting by Odysseus, Eurylochus returned to the camp alone, pale and distraught, with a strange tale to tell.

He and his companions had made their way through the island's forest until they came to a magnificent palace, outside of which lions and mountain wolves roamed at will, but peaceably, although with a questioning, anxious look in their eyes. They seemed to be in a drugged state. There was something deeply sad and unreal about their movements and the way they looked at the men.

Even while Eurylochus and his companions were gazing at these animals in wonder, they could hear indescribably beautiful singing coming from the palace. It was a woman's voice, alluring and haunting. Then the singing ceased, and when one of the men called out, the doors opened and the singer stood in the doorway — a divine being, gloriously beautiful, who smiled and beckoned the men inside.

Eurylochus felt uneasy. It was as though a voice inside was warning him. While his companions surged forward, he hung back, hiding behind a tree, which he then climbed so that he could look down into the main hall of the palace. A strange sight met his eyes. The goddess, surrounded by his men, was serving them wine in abundance. Soon they were swaying drunkenly, their eyes glazed and their senses dulled.

It was then that Circe (for it was she) took her wand and touched each of them in turn. Immediately they got down on all fours and began to grunt like pigs. Their faces grew snouts and their bodies became covered with bristles, until they had turned completely into pigs.

Eurylochus now realised why the animals outside the palace had made him uneasy. They were, in fact, fellow humans, drugged and enchanted by the beautiful witch-goddess. What was to be done?

Odysseus, on hearing this story, set out immediately for the palace. He was making his way through the forest when he was accosted by a beautiful youth wearing golden sandals and carrying a golden wand. This was Hermes, the messenger of the gods, who had been sent to warn Odysseus and tell him how to avoid Circe's spells. Stooping down, Hermes plucked a sprig of herb, known as *moly*, which had a milky flower but roots that were as black as Hades.

If this herb were placed in the drink offered by Circe the drink would lose its potency, Hermes told Odysseus. When the sorceress leaned forward with her wand, Odysseus must make as though to kill her with his sword. Circe would then plead with him to save her life, promising to make love with him if he would only spare her. This Odysseus must do; for no man must refuse the advances of a goddess. Having delivered his message, Hermes flew off, and Odysseus made his way to the palace.

There, everything happened as Hermes had foretold. Circe was more beautiful and more enticing than Odysseus had imagined. Her singing was softly seductive. He knew he was being lured by a sweet enchantress. Stern of will, Odysseus did everything as Hermes had instructed him. When he drew his sword and the sorceress pleaded with him, he bargained with her. "Only if you turn my men back into their normal selves will I let you go, and love you," he told her. "Swear to do this," he insisted.

Circe did as Odysseus demanded. She led him to the sties and opened the gates. As Odysseus's men rushed out, grunting and snuffling, she touched each one of them with her wand. One by one they were restored to their own shape, and were overjoyed at being released from the spell of the enchantress.

Now Circe looked lovingly at Odysseus; and he returned her amorous glances. She bid the adventurer return to his camp and bring the remainder of his comrades to her palace. She promised not to enchant them, but to leave them be. If Odysseus would but love her, she would be content.

After he and his men were bathed and perfumed, and clothed in dazzling garments woven by Circe herself, the company sat down to a feast fit for the gods.

As the evening wore on Circe took Odysseus by the hand and led him from the hall. She was claiming his promise.

For a year Odysseus and his men stayed at the palace of Circe, sated with pleasure. Yet Odysseus knew that he could not forget his wife and homeland forever. When one of his men told him that it was time to go, he knew that it was so. Circe, in tears, begged him to stay, but Odysseus was adamant.

"Go then," Circe told him, "but your way will not be easy. Poseidon will seek to destroy you and Zeus must be appeased. He has declared that you must visit the underworld and survive before you will be allowed to return home."

"No one visits Hades and comes back from the place of the dead," he told her.

"Set sail and go," she insisted. "I will give you a ram and a black ewe. These you must offer up to the gods at the entrance to the underworld. Their blood will conjure up the spirits of the dead. Sacrifice the sheep by fire. Pray to Hades and Persephone, and the spirits will guide you safely through their kingdom. Go, and when your mission is accomplished, return to me to be refreshed. Then you can continue your journey homeward."

All went as Circe had predicted. Odysseus sailed to the land of perpetual night, entered the gloom of the dread underworld and did as he had been told by Circe.

The first spirit he conjured up was Anticleia, his mother, who appeared, wraith-like, before him, then melted back again into the shadow that she now was.

Then Tiresias, the blind prophet and spokesman for the ghosts of Hades, warned Odysseus that his way home to Ithaca would be long and dangerous. Anticleia then reappeared to tell her son that his wife, Penelope, and his son, Telemachus, were still alive and awaiting his return, although Penelope was besieged by suitors who insisted that Odysseus had joined the souls of the departed.

It was with relief, but great sadness, that Odysseus sailed away from black Hades and into the clear waters of the Mediterranean, and back to Aeaea where Circe was eagerly waiting his return.

Circe and her maidens had food prepared for Odysseus and his men, and flagons of refreshing wine. Taking Odysseus by the hand, she drew him aside from the others and looked into his eyes with love, for was she not bearing his child, whom she was to call Telegonus? Some say there were other sons, too, Agrius and Latinus. However that may be, Circe's love for Odysseus was sure and strong — and also wise. Well she knew that she could not expect to hold this bold adventurer forever. So she sighed, then smiled, and warned her lover of the dangers of his homeward voyage, giving him advice which would stand him in good stead in the long days ahead. It was Circe who warned the adventurer against the treacherous Sirens, Daughters of the Muse, Melpomene and the river-god, Achelous. These monsters, half-woman and half-bird, lured sailors to their death on the reef of their island home. But Odysseus, warned by Circe, stopped the ears of his sailors with wax, then had them lash him to the mast of his ship as he sailed past the Sirens' island. Thus he became the only man to hear the Sirens' seductive singing and survive.

Although most storytellers say that Odysseus died "worn out after an easy old age" an Ancient Roman writer, Hyginus, who wrote his *Fabulae* in about 200 AD, tells us that years after Odysseus arrived home, Circe sent Telegonus in search of his father. After he reached the island of Ithaca, Telegonus accidentally killed Odysseus. When he discovered what he had done, he was distraught and overcome with remorse, and took his father's body back to Aeae to be buried, accompanied by Penelope and Telemachus.

Circe's last recorded act was to make Penelope and Telemachus immortal. Then she married Telemachus, while Telegonus married Penelope, who bore him a son, whom they called Italus. These things can happen when mortals share their lives with those whose ancestors dwelt on the heady heights of Mount Olympus.

Medea: A Cruel and Savage Witch

Medea was a daughter of Aeëtes, king of Colchis (a son of Helios, the sun-god) and the youngest of the Oceanides, Idyia, whose name, like Medea's, means "cunning", "knowing". From childhood Medea was entrancingly beautiful, but took after her aunt, Circe, and early became knowledgeable about the magical properties of certain herbs. She became a skilful witch, a devotee of Hecate, and could work miracles for good, but also for evil.

Because of Medea's powerful magic, the goddess Hera brought her to Greece, to the island of Colchis, as part of an elaborate plan conceived by Hera to take revenge on Pelias, king of Iolcus, whom she hated because he refused to honour her with sacrifices.

It was Hera, working through the mind of Pelias, who contrived that Jason, the Argonaut, would be given the quest of bringing the golden fleece from Colchis to Iolcus.

When Jason and his Argonauts reached Colchis and were escorted to the palace, one of the first to greet them was Medea. This is where her story really begins.

With Jason and Medea it was love at first sight, a dire attraction cunningly arranged by Hera, who had ordered Aphrodite to send her son, Eros, to pierce Medea with his arrow. Not only did Medea fall instantly and violently in love with Jason, but he returned her passion as ardently as she gave him hers. Aphrodite, who knew that Jason would want Medea to help him outwit her father and to carry off the golden fleece, appeared before Medea in the guise of her aunt, Circe, the enchantress, to persuade Medea that all would be well. She must follow where her heart led.

So it was that, with Medea's help, Jason was able to complete the seemingly impossible tasks set for him by Aeëtes before he could even venture into the sacred grove where the golden fleece hung from the branches of a great ilex tree, guarded by a dragon who slept neither by day nor by night.

Medea knew well that even if Jason succeeded in winning the golden fleece her father would slay the Argonauts in the dead of night. To save Jason she must leave the island with him.

"If I help you gain the fleece will you marry me?" she asked the handsome Argonaut.

"Willingly," he gave answer. "Just as soon as we are able." That very night Medea led the way through the forest to the grove. Again she used her sorcery and cunning. With the dragon lulled to sleep by Orpheus and with Jason protected by her magic ointment, the golden fleece was his. Jason merely had to climb along the dragon's coils and reach up to take the treasure.

Quickly the lovers sped through the night to the waiting *Argo*, where Apsyrtus, Medea's young brother, was waiting to join them. The Argonauts hoisted their sails only minutes before Aeëtes arrived at the shore in pursuit, determined not to lose the fleece, and to do away with Jason. But it was too late. The *Argo* was already leaving Colchis behind. Jason and Medea were safe — for a while, at least.

It was now that the dark and evil heart of Medea began to have its way. Perhaps she wanted Jason bound to her by guilt, perhaps she wanted to be free of all memories of her life on Colchis. Whatever her motives, Apsyrtus must die.

Legend differs as to the details of his death, but certainly Jason was far from blameless. Perhaps it is true that Medea lured Apsyrtus to a lonely island, then tricked Jason into killing him; for ancient stories tell how Jason not only dismembered the corpse of Apsyrtus, but also that he tossed the pieces into the sea from the *Argo*, to delay the pursuing Colchians, who were honour bound to rescue the floating fingers and toes for burial.

Both Jason and Medea knew that they were guilty of treachery and murder, and that the gods must be propitiated for their misdeeds. Moreover, the prow of the *Argo* began to speak, revealing to the Argonauts that Jason and Medea were murderers. So it was that they visited the island of Aeaea, where Circe ritually cleansed them before she knew just how treacherous they had been. Although it was too late to withhold purification, Circe called down a curse upon the pair, so that their paths were forever to be dogged by tragedy.

Now Medea formed another plan to escape from her father's men, who were still in pursuit of her and her lover. She and Jason must be married on the Phaeacians' island of Drepone so that the Phaeacian king, Alcinous, would guarantee their safety.

In a cave, forever to be known as Medea's Cave, the couple celebrated their marriage. After a short stay they continued their voyage, which would take them eventually back to Iolcus where the usurper king, Pelias, was waiting for Jason to return with the golden fleece.

Many adventures awaited Jason and Medea along the way. When the *Argo* was washed up on the shore in a storm off the island of Syrtis, Jason had the Argonauts carry the ship on their backs. The crew trudged across the sands to Lake Tritonis, where Triton, the water-god, helped them get back to the sea and relaunch the ship.

Off the island of Crete they were challenged by Talos, a giant bronze robot fashioned by Hephaestus, which guarded the island for King Minos by running around it three times a day and hurling rocks at anyone who tried to land. Anyone who managed to set foot on the island, Talos would burn to death. But Talos had a weak spot. In his ankle, under very tough skin, was lodged a nail which acted as a stopper in the vein on which his life depended. Medea called her magic into play and she bewitched Talos with false visions that led him into a dangerous, rocky part of the island. As he stumbled, Talos grazed his ankle badly, the nail became unstuck, and the creature bled to death. The Argonauts were then free to disembark, spend the night on Crete, and set out for Iolcus the next day.

When Jason returned home in triumph with the fabled golden fleece he did not really expect Pelias to hand over the kingdom as he had promised. He knew too well the false heart of the usurper king. Yet Jason also knew that he and the Argonauts were not strong enough to take the kingdom by force. When Pelias refused Jason's right to rule, Jason turned to his wife, Medea, for help.

Medea had no problem thinking of a scheme to conquer Pelias without resorting to arms. This was what Hera had anticipated, and it was all part of her cunning scheme to have her revenge on Pelias.

It so happened that Jason's father Aeson, although old and feeble, was still alive, and living at Iolcus. Moved by his father's pitiful weakness, Jason begged Medea to use her magic to take some of his own remaining years and give them to his father, and so rejuvenate him. Medea was indignant. "That I will never do," she assured her husband, "but I can help your father, if you will trust me implicitly."

With Jason's consent Medea set to work. In a secret and elaborate ritual, after scouring the countryside at night for certain herbs, she slit the old man's throat, then filled Aeson's veins with a brew from the herbs which she had boiled in a pot. As the magic began to work Aeson's wrinkled skin smoothed out, his eyes grew clear, his speech lost all trace of age. He was young and sprightly once more.

The daughters of Pelias who were present at the ritual were astounded. Never had they witnessed such a miracle! Could not Medea perform the same wonder-

working magic on their father? Of course, but no ritual took exactly the same course. The daughters must prepare their father for the rejuvenating transfusion by chopping him up and boiling him in a cauldron.

This the daughters refused to do, as Medea knew they would. Her plan was to convince them that what she proposed would indeed work.

Into the simmering pot she plunged the pieces of an old ram which she cut up before their eyes. After incantations over the brew, the witch pulled out from the pot the vision of a lamb which appeared to frisk about in her hands.

The daughters were struck with awe and wonder. After a quick consultation they seized their father, Pelias, ran him through with their swords, then chopped him up and flung the pieces into the pot. To their dismay and horror Pelias failed to re-emerge alive, let alone rejuvenated.

Medea was in command of the situation. At her signal the Argonauts marched into the city and took over with little opposition from the demoralised soldiers. Hera had had her revenge on Pelias, and Medea had been her instrument.

But Hera now withdrew her patronage from Jason and Medea, and the couple, because of their crime, were forced to flee from Iolcus, where Acastus, the son of Pelias, was stirring up antagonism against them. Jason and his witch-wife now fled to Corinth, where they were made welcome by the king, Creon, who knew well the exploits of the leader of the Argonauts.

For ten years Jason and Medea lived peacefully in Corinth. Medea bore Jason two sons. On the surface all was well. But although Creon and the Corinthians were pleased to have Jason living in their city like a king, they were less pleased to have a witch, who to them was also a barbarian, dwelling among them.

At length Creon summoned Jason into his presence and said to him: "I will speak plainly. If you are prepared to divorce your wife, Medea, I will give you my daughter, Glauce, in marriage. When I die, you will inherit the throne; but your sons by Medea must not have any claim to it. So they must be banished from the kingdom."

Slowly Jason nodded his assent, then spoke. "It shall be as you propose, my lord. It grieves me, but it must be done. I give you my word." So Jason and Glauce were betrothed.

Medea was enraged. With loud, wailing cries and oaths she called on the gods to witness what recompense she must receive from Jason. For days she fasted and gave herself over to abandoned grief. She refused to speak or to eat or to sleep. She was like a tigress prowling through the corridors of the palace. "Would that I were dead!" she cried. Her moanings filled the passageways and her sighs and wailing echoed through the porch from her chamber.

But Medea was never faint of heart. Her fury begat in her a lust for revenge. "Jason will not get away with this," she murmured to herself. "If I can't have him, Glauce never will." Slowly, a plot began to form in her mind.

"Now shall I triumph over my foes. This is my plan. One of my household shall I send to Jason, and will entreat him to come to me. When he comes, soft words will I speak, saying, 'What is your will is my will. It is well. This royal marriage is to your advantage, and well thought through.' Then I'll petition him that our sons can stay. Not that I would leave my sons to be badly treated on foreign soil, but I will use them as part of my plan. I will send them bearing gifts to the bride, so that they may not be banished. Robes, fine-spun, and a golden diadem will I send her. If she receives and puts on the robes and my ornaments, she shall die wretchedly, as will all who touch her. For I shall anoint my gifts with drugs so deadly that none may wear them, and live. Then I will slay my children. No one shall pluck them from my hand. Then, having brought ruin upon Jason's house, I shall flee the land. He shall live on, never more seeing the sons I bore him; never begetting a son by his new bride — that wretch, foredoomed to die in agony by my doing. Let no one call me weak or spiritless — rather, as grim to my foes as I am kindly to my friends. Most glorious is the life of such as I."

But first Medea tried to reason with Jason, reminding him of all that they had achieved together. In truth he had to admit to this, but he taunted his wife with being a foreigner, a barbarian, whom he had introduced to the glory that was Greece.

Medea determined to have her revenge. She put her plan into action. Her sons bore the poisoned clothes and ornaments to Glauce who was in her bower; and who took the rich-wrought robes and clad herself, circling her ringlets with the golden crown, arranging her tresses in the golden mirror, smiling at herself as she did so. Slowly, with mincing steps, she began her passage down the hallway, proudly eyeing herself from neck to hem as she paraded.

Suddenly she began to stagger. Scarcely did she have time to make her way to a nearby couch before her limbs began to tremble. She grew deathly pale, drops of perspiration rolled down her face; she began to froth at the mouth. Then a long, loud scream of horror broke from her lips. Her father heard it and ran along the corridors to her aid. He arrived to find Glauce clutching at the diadem, which seemed to burn like red-hot coals into her head. Her flesh was aflame with pain from the robes. Blood streamed down her face, and as her father held her in his arms she died a hideously painful death.

Her father cried out and clasped her body to his own frail limbs, moaning and saying, "O my unhappy child, what demon has devoured you? Who makes your body into a graveyard? Ah, would that I could die with you!"

Those were Creon's last words. The robes which he clutched so firmly to his bosom had done their dreadful work. He too had joined his daughter at the threshold of Hades. Medea's revenge had begun to work.

There was more yet. In an inner chamber Medea drew her sword upon her unfortunate children. Their cries brought Jason hurrying to the door of the chamber from which their blood was seeping. In a frenzy Jason called out for vengeance, "Shall she, who has murdered the lords of the land escape unscathed from these halls? For myself I care not, but for my sons. I who have been wronged should avenge that wrong. Burst in the bolts with all speed, my men. Force the hinges! Let me view this twofold horror — the dead children and her! Let me avenge them with her blood."

Even as he spoke Medea appeared on the palace roof, in a chariot drawn by winged dragons. Looking down at Jason she called with scorn in her voice; "Why shake the doors and unlock them, seeking your dead sons, and me who wrought their death? Stop trying. If you want anything of me, say it. Your hand will never touch me again. This chariot has been sent by my father's sire, the Sun. It shall save me from even you!"

Taunting Jason with having killed his sons by his own lust, Medea was borne out of sight in her chariot, and Jason was left alone, undone and lamenting.

Drawn in her grandfather's chariot, Medea fled from Corinth to Athens, where she immediately sought out Aegeus, the king of that city. Only a short time before, Aegeus had visited Corinth, and Medea, already with fear for the future in her heart, had worked on Aegeus, getting him to promise that should she ever come to Athens he would give her his patronage. In return she promised to use her magic to ensure that he would have the children he so badly desired. Although Aegeus was unaware of it, he had already fathered a child by Aethra in Troezen: a boy called Theseus.

Now Aegeus saw in Medea the wife who could bear him a son and heir. So he married her; and Medea did have a son by him, whom she called Medus.

Years passed, with little to tell. Then Theseus, who had grown to manhood, appeared in Athens at the court of Aegeus, who knew not that this young hero was his son. And Theseus knew not that Aegeus was his father.

But Medea did, and fearing lest Theseus dispute the claim of Medus to the throne of Athens, should it become known that Theseus was the king's son, she persuaded Aegeus that Theseus meant to kill him.

So Theseus was dispatched to fetch the dangerous bull of Marathon. The young Cretan boldly accomplished his task, and that night the king arranged a banquet prepared by Medea. The witch now had yet another plan. She would slip Theseus a cup of poisoned wine, and she would be free of yet another possibly dangerous rival.

It was as Theseus was taking the cup from Medea's hands that Aegeus saw that the young man was wearing his, Aegeus's own sword and sandals, which could only mean that this young man was his son. Aegeus struck the poisoned cup from Theseus's hand and claimed him as his successor to the throne of Athens.

Medea was once again sent into exile. This time her son, Medus, went with her.

They first stopped at the city of Absorus, which was overrun with deadly serpents, and where the citizens begged Medea to help them against the plague. Once more Medea used her magic, and confined the serpents in the tomb of her brother, Apsyrtus. From that time on, if one slithered outside the tomb, it died immediately.

From Absorus, Medea sent Medus ahead of her to Colchis, where Perses, who had killed his brother, Aeëtes, now ruled. Perses immediately threw Medus into prison, as he had been warned in prophecy that a descendant of Aeëtes was destined to kill him. In vain did Medus disclaim any relationship to his grandfather, stating instead that he was a Corinthian, Hippotes, the son of Creon. He languished in prison, but the gods knew of his plight, and the Colchian crops failed as a result of the injustice. The land and its people were in misery.

It was then that Medea arrived in Colchis, impersonating a priestess of Artemis. She promised that she would end the drought if the imprisoned youth was given over to her to be killed as part of her rites. Perses agreed, and Medus was given over to his mother.

When Medea discovered that the young man was her own son, she gave him a sword, telling him to kill Perses with it. Medus did as she instructed, thus avenging his grandfather, Aeëtes, and fulfilling the prophecy.

Medus took the throne of Colchis and later conquered the land to the east, and named it Media after himself — the land of the Medes.

There is no record in legend of Medea's death. Perhaps she still lives on in another guise. In one tradition she became the consort of Achilles in the Elysian Fields, while in another she was worshipped as a goddess. But whatever way, the name Medea will always be associated with treachery and guile, a name to strike fear into the hearts of all people who have ever practised deceit.

Guanyin:
The Goddess of Mercy

As Mary is revered by Christians so Guanyin (or Kuan Yin) is the guiding spirit of the Buddhist faith.

This Chinese Goddess of Mercy is so called because of the legend which tells that as she was about to enter Heaven she heard a cry of pain and anguish rising from the earth beneath her. Moved by compassion, she paused as her feet touched the glorious threshold. So she is known as the one who hears the cry and prayers of the world. She symbolises mercy.

Guanyin was usually thought of as a male god until the twelfth century. Originally Guanyin was an Indian Buddhist deity who was introduced to China by Buddhist missionaries travelling from India via Tibet. Perhaps the Chinese tendency to equate mercy with femininity caused the gradual change from male to female. By the twelfth century Guanyin was generally represented as a woman.

The Goddess of Mercy was worshipped as a saviour and protectress, especially of sailors, and eclipsed the Empress of Heaven, a female Neptune, as the patroness of storm-tossed seamen. In times of drought she was believed to have brought rain from the hills. Where other gods were feared, she was loved. Their countenance may have been black and scornful, hers was gentle and radiant. Her image was found in numerous homes and there was a chapel to her honour in most temples. She was the patron goddess of mothers, but the protectress and comforter of all in times of sorrow. She is still worshipped today.

Her throne is said to be on the island of P'u T'o off the coast of central China, to which she came floating as a waterlily. She is the epitome of Chinese beauty. When one has evil thoughts, a prayer to Guanyin will drive them away. Anger and malice can be overcome by calling on her name.

Tradition also has it that Guanyin was originally an ancient Chinese princess called Miao Shan. But first of all there was her father . . .

In the time of the Golden Heavenly Dynasty in China there was a king called Miao Chuang whose queen was known as Pao Tê. They had been married for many years without having a male heir. This was a source of great grief to them. So the king sent fifty Buddhist and Taoist priests to the God of Hua Shan, the sacred mountain, to pray for seven days and nights asking pardon for all the previous wrongs which the king had committed, and begging for a son. These envoys took with them many rare and valuable gifts, and for seven days and nights the temple rang with the sound of drums, bells and other instruments. Then the king and the queen came themselves to offer prayers and sacrifices.

But the God of Hua Shan knew that the king had no heir because of a three-year-long, bloody war, which he had waged in order to gain his kingdom. However, he made this concession. There were three brothers Shih who were waiting to be reincarnated after having lived a life of piety and good works, but who had died showing a lack of compassion for others who were wrongdoers. So the god was prepared to take into account their past good life and pardon their crime by giving them the opportunity to be reborn, but of the female sex, in the womb of Pao Tê, the queen. In their new life they would have an opportunity to atone for their lack of compassion, and save many souls. The god ordered the Spirit of the North Pole to free the three captive souls and take them to the palace of Miao Chuang, where in three years' time they would be born as females to the queen, Pao Tê.

The king anxiously awaited the birth of an heir. A year after his visit to the temple his wife bore him a baby daughter whom they called Miao Ch'ing. A year later a second daughter was born, Miao Yin. Another year went by and a third daughter was born. The king was furiously angry at not having received a son this time but named his new daughter, Miao Shan.

From the moment of her birth Miao Shan displayed all the attributes of a good Buddhist. She was kind, gentle, modest and loving. She refused to eat meat and always had compassion on anything weaker or smaller than herself. When she was but a tiny girl she confided in her sisters that her only ambition was to be a nun and to live a secluded life on top of a high mountain where she could attain perfection.

It was not long before the king found wise and suitable husbands for his two eldest daughters, leaving only Miao Shan unmarried. Miao Chuang explained to his daughter that as soon as he could find a man rich enough, famous enough and worthy of ruling a kingdom she should marry him.

"But father," explained Miao Shan, "although it would hurt me deeply to offend you by objecting to your wishes, I must tell you that I do not wish ever to marry. I wish only to attain perfection and Buddhahood, and to do good to all mankind."

The king was furious. "No royal daughter of mine will be a nun. Give up these

51

foolish ideas. I'll soon find you a suitable academician or a military first graduate. You'll marry him and that will be an end of your nonsense."

The two of them argued to and fro. At last Miao Shan said in desperation, "If I must be made to marry, let it be to a physician. Then I will be able to help in the healing of the poor, the needy, the aged and the infirm. So grant me this, I implore you, and I will marry today."

"That you won't," replied her father. "You will marry whom I choose, otherwise you will be no daughter of mine. I will cast you out."

"If that is your will, father, then it must be so," said Miao Shan sadly.

At this the king's countenance became firmly set, and he looked long and hard at his daughter. Then turning away with an impatient sigh he clapped his hands to summon the officer in charge of the palace guard.

"Take this wretched daughter of mine from my presence," he said. "All she wants in life is to be a nun. Well, take her to the queen's garden and give her a taste of the solitary life. Let her suffer the pangs of hunger, let her even perish with cold. I no longer care what becomes of her. She is both disobedient and ungrateful."

So Miao Shan was stripped of her royal finery and banished to the garden to live the frugal life of a holy hermit. This suited the girl admirably. There she had peace, and time to spend on her devotions. Nirvana, the highest state of spiritual bliss, seemed so much closer, and she was content. Her diet of dew and garden plants satisfied her well.

When the king and the queen saw that their daughter was determined to lead the life of a recluse they talked the matter over and sent messengers to her, pleading with her once again to listen to their entreaties, and to marry the man of their choice.

Miao Shan sent back word that she was more convinced than ever not to marry, and begged her parents to allow her to go to the Nunnery of the White Bird, where five hundred Buddhist nuns devoted their lives to the study of doctrine and the pursuit of perfection.

"Very well, let her go," said the king, and immediately sent word to the superior of the nunnery, instructing her to dissuade his daughter from her purpose, but if she remained adamant to give her the most menial and distasteful tasks in the community.

That is exactly what happened. When the princess arrived, the other nuns paid her due respect as the daughter of the king. But she told them that all she wanted was to be one of them, and an equal. The superior took her aside and counselled her to return home and comply with her parents' wishes.

"It can never be," was all that Miao Shan would say.

So the superior directed the princess to the kitchen where she was to scrub and scour, prepare the rice for the community's meals and serve her fellow nuns.

This made Miao Shan happy indeed. When the superior observed her kneeling before the Buddha and offering her work to his glory she was moved with pity and admiration for the girl.

What is more, the poor girl's prayers and devotions ascended to the gods in heaven, to the master of heaven, the Jade Emperor, who dispatched benevolent spirits to assist the girl with her work, so that her tasks were quickly accomplished. A sea-dragon dug her a well, a tiger fetched firewood, birds gathered fruit and vegetables from the garden. This gave Miao Shan more time for prayer and meditation.

When the superior saw what was happening, and when she realised that now the great bell of the nunnery tolled nightly as though of its own accord, she knew that she was witnessing a miracle. In haste she sent word to the king, begging him to recall his recalcitrant daughter.

Miao Chuang was now obsessed by what he perceived to be his daughter's perversity. In a temper he sent off a corps of his soldiers with orders to destroy the nunnery by fire. Let his daughter perish along with the rest of the nuns.

As the fires kindled by the soldiers leapt along the walls of the nunnery, the terrified women railed at Miao Shan for bringing this dreadful thing to pass.

Miao Shan sank to her knees and implored the aid of the Great Sovereign of the Universe, humbly acknowledging that she it was who was responsible for the doom which hung over her sisters. Then she loosened a long bamboo hairpin from her hair and pricked the roof of her mouth with it. As the blood flowed and filled her mouth she tilted back her head and spat a living stream of blood toward heaven. Instantly great thunderclouds gathered above the nunnery and a torrent of rain fell, dousing the fires completely.

The nuns fell to their knees and gave thanks to heaven and to Miao Shan. But the superior sent word to the king telling him all that had come to pass. Miao Chuang was beside himself with rage and gave orders to have his daughter returned to him in chains, and to have her beheaded on arrival.

Although the queen intervened and persuaded the king to give his daughter another chance, Miao Shan stood firm. Execution would only hasten the journey of her soul to another world. She would accept her fate.

The king gave the order for her beheading. The executioner stood ready. It was as though the world stopped still. A great darkness spread across the land. As the executioner's sword flashed downward a great light shone from the body of the victim, and the sword shattered in two. When a spear was thrust at her, it, too, fell to pieces. The King gave orders that his daughter be strangled with a silken cord. It was at the moment of her death that a tiger, sent by the Jade Emperor, who watched over the girl from heaven, sprang forward and bore her dead body into the pine-forests.

While Miao Shan's body was being carried away her soul had migrated to a desolate place where nothing grew, no creature moved and from whence there came no sound at all.

"Where am I?" her soul cried. "What terrible curse has come upon me?"

Even as her thoughts ascended, a young man dressed in a heavenly blue tunic carrying a banner appeared. He addressed the soul of the girl thus;

"I am commanded by the king of hells to accompany you to the eighteen infernal regions. Your determination to remain single and devote your life to piety in spite of all threats against you has impressed the gods of the ten hells. You have nothing to fear. Just come with me."

So Miao Shan was led through all the infernal regions to the gods of the ten hells.

"We have heard that when you pray, evil disperses as your goodness shines through the darkness of sin. Let us hear you pray," they told her.

"Gladly. But before I do, I beg of you that all the lost souls in these infernal regions be released from their chains and be given leave to hear me pray."

And so it happened. As the maiden prayed, shafts of light played around the spot where she knelt, soft music filled that terrible place and hell became a paradise. Where there was despair there was hope, lamentations turned to cries of joy, and gladness entered the abode of sorrow. The souls of the condemned rejoiced as they were reprieved and set free.

The gods of the ten hells, however, were not pleased.

"If there is to be any justice in the universe then hell cannot become a heaven. This saintly maiden must go."

Then the kings of hell made obeisance to Miao Shan, and the young man dressed in the heavenly blue tunic conducted her soul across the Styx Bridge to the pine-forests, where body and soul were reunited in the upper world.

As she looked anew at the world around her, Miao Shan sighed regretfully. The memory of those tortured souls in hell was still with her, and she longed for perfection for herself and the opportunity to bring wholeness and harmony to those whose lives were in tatters.

Even as she thought on these things the lonely figure of a handsome man approached, and he began to converse with her. After a little while he said, "I see that we are two solitary souls, yet we think and feel alike. Why do we not marry and spend our days together?"

"Sir, you know not what you ask. Why should I, who have been to hell and back because of my refusal to marry the man of my father's choice, now couple with you? No, No. I can never give myself to any man. My life is dedicated to renunciation and perfection."

The man looked at her and a soft and gentle smile spread across his countenance.

"You speak well, my daughter. For am I not the Buddha of the West, and have

I not been testing your virtue — a test which you have passed without shadow of doubt. So now I invite you to reside in the ancient monastery of Hsiang Shan, where Immortals dwell. For it is there that you will be able to attain the highest perfection."

As he spoke, the Buddha handed Miao Shan a peach and bade her eat it. "The flesh of this peach will stave off hunger and thirst. Old age and death will never claim you, and you will become immortal." So saying, the Buddha disappeared from Miao Shan's view.

The maiden ate the peach thoughtfully, then set out through the forests in the direction of P'u T'o Island where was situated the monastery of Hsiang Shan. It was a long, hard road to travel, and just when it seemed that Miao Shan's strength was failing her, a tiger sprang out from behind a rock, roaring ferociously.

Seeing a look of fright appear on the girl's face, the tiger spoke, "Do not be afraid. I am not a real tiger. I am the guardian of the soil of Hsiang Shan and have come to conduct you there. Jump on my back, and all will be well."

Miao Shan did so and in the twinkling of an eye she was conveyed to the monastery on the island of P'u T'o, which was to become her home for the next nine years.

By the end of that time the daughter of Miao Chuang had attained the peak of perfection. When she wished it, her soul could withdraw from her body, and always it was at the service of others. Her perfect life became the inspiration of all creatures near and far, and she became regarded as the queen of all virtue.

Then on the nineteenth day of the eleventh moon, a great concourse of dignitaries assembled on the island P'u T'o. The dragon king of the western sea was there, the gods of the five sacred mountains, all the emperor-saints, officials of the Ministry of Time, the heavenly functionaries in charge of wind, rain, thunder and lightning were also there along with the three causes, the five saints, the eight immortals and the ten gods of the hells — all gathered for the most solemn of ceremonies. With all that vast company attending, Miao Shan took her seat on the lotus throne, and the assembled dignitaries and gods proclaimed her a Buddha, and queen of heaven and earth. A worthy maiden and a virtuous young man were to be appointed to protect and serve her in the temple, and a search was begun to find companions worthy of the celestial queen.

In the course of the search it was reported to Miao Shan that a certain young priest who had become a hermit and who was a novice in the art of perfection was seeking her aid in his quest for wholeness, harmony and radiance. He was journeying toward her and had reached a lonely mountain peak.

Then Miao Shan instructed the Immortals to disguise themselves as brigands and besiege the mountain with brandished torches. She herself appeared at the young priest's side as the horde advanced. With a cry for help she sprang forward, appeared to miss her footing and rolled down the mountainside to the

56

gorge below. Without hesitation the young priest, Shan Ts'ai, sprang after her with tears in his eyes. But although his body was dashed, lifeless, on the rocks, Miao Shan, who knew the courage of his heart, transformed him so that his soul could rise and fly to be beside her as companion and protector throughout time.

It was some time after this that Miao Shan, with her gift of spiritual sight, saw the son of the dragon king of the southern sea swimming through the waves in the form of a carp. While she was watching she saw him caught in the net of a fisherman, and offered for sale at the local market. Miao Shan sent her servant, Shan Ts'ai, to buy the carp and to free it in the ocean by the island of P'u T'o. When the dragon king's son returned to his father and told him what had happened, the dragon king in gratitude sent Miao Shan a beautiful luminous pearl, so that she could see in the dark, and pray by its light. This gift was carried to Miao Shan by the dragon king's granddaughter, who begged to be allowed to dwell with Miao Shan to pursue wisdom and piety. So Lung Nü was accepted as a devotee. She called Shan Ts'ai "brother", and he called her "sister".

Now after King Miao Chuang had burned down the Nunnery of the White Bird in order to kill his daughter, the heavenly king consulted the register of the living and the dead to see how much longer this wretched ruler had left on earth. When he saw that the king still had twenty years to reign he sent for the God of Epidemics, who in punishment for Miao Chuang's crimes, brought down on the king a plague of boils, which caused him grievous bodily pain that tortured him relentlessly day and night.

The most famous court physicians could bring no relief. The king's suffering only increased, and he became so desperate that he issued a promise of succession to his throne to anyone who could heal him.

Revelation of her father's suffering came to Miao Shan, and she visited the palace in the disguise of a priest-doctor. She wore the physician's headdress and straw shoes; and attached to her girdle were pills and other potions contained in a gourd. Presenting herself to the palace guard she begged for an audience with the queen. After her time with the queen she was admitted to the presence of the king, whom she examined gravely, telling him that his condition was not incurable.

"However," she said, "the remedy is not easy to come by, for it is not found in any pharmacy, and it is not for sale."

The irritable king sent her from his presence, too impatient to talk in riddles. But that night in a dream he was told that only this priest-doctor could work a remedy. So the next day he summoned his disguised daughter to his bedside and demanded to know the treatment.

"Only the eye and the hand of a living person can cure you," she advised him solemnly. "These must be compounded into an ointment, which, when applied will prove to be a remedy."

Although the king was sceptical his pain was so great that he was prepared to go to any lengths to put an end to it. "Where can such a remedy be found?" he demanded. "Is there anyone in my kingdom who is prepared to make this sacrifice for me?"

"Your majesty must send his ministers to the monastery of Hsiang Shan at once," Miao Shan assured him. "There the remedy may be obtained, provided the ministers follow faithfully the Buddhist rules of abstinence."

The king dispatched his ministers immediately, but his two sons-in-law were secretly very upset. They were counting on the king dying from his disease, so that they could seize the throne and rule in his stead. They had, as an accomplice, an unscrupulous courtier called Ho Lin. The three villains then hatched an evil plot.

That night an assassin named Su Ta was to plunge his knife into the body of the priest-doctor, while Ho Lin was to administer poison prepared by the sons-in-law to the king. The poison would be given to the king in a bowl of innocent-looking soup.

Now Miao Shan had returned to the monastery at Hsiang Shan, but with her supernatural gifts she was able to have the body of the priest-doctor remain at the palace. From this body she saw the traitorous sons-in-law preparing the poisoned soup. She immediately sent a guardian spirit to render the poison harmless and to bind the assassin. Thus it was that when Ho Lin appeared at midnight with the soup the spirit dashed the bowl to the ground. At the same instant as Su Ta was plunging his knife into the heart of the priest-doctor the assassin was bound by a supernatural power.

When Su Ta was found by the king's guards the next morning alongside the wounded body of the priest-doctor, he was questioned, then tortured until he confessed every detail of the plot.

Miao Chuang's wrath could not be contained. He ordered the immediate execution of his sons-in-law and had his daughters imprisoned in the palace.

Meanwhile the king's ministers had arrived at the monastery of Hsiang Shan and were shown into the presence of Miao Shan. With due ceremony they delivered the king's message, telling of his terrible affliction and begging for the gruesome remedy that the priest-doctor had described.

"It shall be as you wish," Miao Shan told them. "Tomorrow you must come to me, first having sharpened a knife with which to perform the necessary ritual."

The next day when the ministers were brought before her, Miao Shan instructed them to cut off her left hand and gouge out her left eye. The ministers drew back in horror and would have gone away, but Miao Shan insisted so urgently that at last the dreadful deed was done. As the blood splashed red to the ground, the sweet smell of incense filled the air and heavenly music was heard throughout the monastery. The severed hand and the eye were placed on a golden platter, and the ministers returned to their king bearing their precious burden.

Back at the palace the queen was waiting for the ingredients of the cure. By her side was the priest-doctor who helped the queen pound the hand and the eye to ointment, with which the king's left side was then anointed. Even as the unguent was being spread, the boils subsided and the terrible pain eased, then ceased. But only on the left side. The king's right side was still inflamed, and was filled with excruciating pain.

"Is there no complete cure?" he moaned in desperation.

"Only the right eye and the right hand of your benefactor can achieve that cure," affirmed the priest-doctor.

"Then fetch them," commanded the king, and the ministers were again sent off to Hsiang Shan. There they were brought before Miao Shan in her mutilated form, who commanded them to complete their work and return with the ingredients of the cure.

When they delivered their precious cargo to the queen and the priest-doctor, the queen started forward with a terrible cry. On the back of the hand was a black mark which she recognised as her daughter's. But even as she was crying out the priest-doctor was preparing the ointment. Again, while it was still being applied to the king's right side the cure was completed. The king sprang up, free of pain, healed and happy. The great joy that filled his heart turned to wonder and admiration as he looked at the priest-doctor. "Let him be known henceforth as the Priest of the Brilliant Eye," he commanded. "Ask, and whatever reward you wish shall be yours."

"My lord," said Miao Shan in the priest-doctor's guise, "I ask nothing but that you promise henceforth to rule your kingdom with justice, righteousness and love. For my part, I am a wandering spirit, and I beg leave to be allowed to go upon my way."

As the priest-doctor was speaking, a cloud descended from heaven. The priest-doctor approached until the cloud lifted his body skyward. As the cloud ascended a voice was heard saying, "I am a humble teacher from the west. My mission was to cure the king's illness and that mission is now accomplished. Praise Buddha."

Witnesses to this miracle said, "The priest was the living Buddha. He returns to heaven." And they fell on their faces in worship.

But now the queen was wailing and moaning. She could not erase from her mind the vision of the hand, which she knew in her heart belonged to her daughter. She tried to tell the king what she had seen.

The king summoned his ministers and began to question them about the saint who had yielded up hands and eyes on his behalf.

"She bore the appearance of your dead daughter, Miao Shan," they assured him. "But even as the blood flowed from her severed hands and the sockets of her eyes, her face was radiant with happiness," they said.

"Go at once to the monastery of Hsiang Shan," the king commanded. "I myself will make a pilgrimage to the island as soon as it can be arranged."

So it was that Miao Chuang and the queen Pao Tê, journeyed as pilgrims to Hsiang Shan. At last they entered the temple to offer incense. Before them on the altar sat Miao Shan with wounded sockets for eyes and limbs without hands streaming blood. The queen fell into a deep swoon and the king smote his chest and cried out.

Miao Shan reached out her mutilated body to comfort them, and told them all that had befallen her since the fire at the Nunnery of the White Bird.

In anguish the king prostrated himself before his daughter, beating his head upon the ground. "My sin has been great. See the bitterness of heart of one who was without mercy, and who to cure his ills brought about the deformation of his true and loving daughter."

While he was yet speaking the form and face of Miao Shan was transfigured and she was whole again, her face radiant and her eyes shining gently. She descended from the altar and moved toward her father and her mother, hands outstretched.

They, in turn, moved toward her and clasped her in their joint embrace. All three wept.

"Will you now force me to marry?" she asked her father softly.

"No more, no more," replied her father. "You have walked the paths of righteousness and achieved perfection. Henceforth I join you in that path. Pray that I, too, may achieve wholeness."

Then Miao Chuang abdicated the throne and he and his family set out to walk the humble road to perfection. The king of heaven saw them and knew their hearts. Filled with a holy joy, he sent this message to earth: "From this day forward, Miao Shan, you shall be known as Guanyin the Very Merciful, Compassionate Saviour of the Afflicted, the Miraculous and Always Helpful Protectress of Mortals. From your high and precious lotus-flower throne you shall rule the Southern Seas and the island of P'u T'o."

By the decree of the king of heaven the virtue of Miao Shan made atonement for her father's previous sins and Miao Chuang was raised in dignity to the Virtuous Conquering P'u-sa, Surveyor of Mortals. Queen Pao Tê was endowed with the title of P'u-sa of Ten Thousand Virtues, Surveyor of Illustrious Women. The two sisters of Miao Shan were allowed to progress toward true perfection.

Shan Ts'ai became known as the Golden Youth, and Lung Nü as the Jade Maiden.

To this day Miao Shan remains the protectress of mortals and queen of the sea. The incense of her presence fills all the heavenly places.

Rahab and the Fall of Jericho

The name of Rahab was well known in and beyond the fair but strongly fortified city of Jericho, which reached up proudly from the western plain of the Jordan River in ancient Canaan. Jericho, the city of palm trees, as it was known, could claim to be the oldest walled city in the world. And high on its walls stood the house of Rahab, the prostitute, renowned throughout the land for her beauty, and desired by many men. In the legends of the Jews Rahab is said to be one of the four most beautiful women in history. For all her wanton ways she was generous of spirit and a shrewd woman, better to have as a friend than an enemy.

At the time of her life when Rahab's beauty was at its height the Israelites, who had been led by Moses out of slavery from Egypt and who had wandered for forty years in the desert, were camped by the mouth of the Jordan. Moses, their leader and prophet, had died within sight of Canaan, the land promised to them by their God, Yahweh. The thirty days of mourning for Moses were over, the hearts of the Israelites were aflame with ardour for Yahweh, and they had a new leader, Joshua, the son of Nun. Joshua was a young and vigorous warrior who was determined to lead his people into Canaan, the Promised Land, the land flowing with milk and honey, there to rest after their long years of wandering in the wilderness. There they could worship freely the God who had gone before them through the desert at every stage of their long journey, a pillar of cloud by day, and by night a fire which shone within the cloud.

Now Joshua knew that if the Israelites were to occupy Canaan they must first conquer Jericho — a campaign that would take all his military skill and personal cunning. So he summoned two of his most trusted men to his tent. "Disguise yourselves as Canaanites and go to Jericho. I want you to spy out the land. Find out the strength of the city's defences, how many armed men there are, and the condition of their weapons. There is a woman of the city named Rahab. Her house stands on the city wall. Go to her, for in her house you will learn all that goes on in the city and be able to observe the comings and goings of the soldiers."

Well equipped for their sojourn, the two spies crossed the Jordan and trekked across the burning plain, until at evening they came to the oasis city with its cypress groves, its vineyards and bowers of orange trees. From the hills flowed a clear stream of cooling water, to form a pool where fish darted in the depths and by which the birds gathered in the trees and shrubs in the cool of the day. Looking up, the two men saw the lights come on in the house of Rahab. As Joshua had commanded, they posed as travellers, seeking to spend the night at her house.

Rahab, for her part, raised the lamp the better to regard them, then admitted the spies to her house where she herself served them supper.

Unbeknown to Rahab and to Joshua's men, the chief of the city's watch had seen through the disguise of the spies as they passed through the main city gate, and had followed them to Rahab's house. When the watchman made his report to the king, the king was mightily angered and sent a messenger at once to Rahab saying, "The two men who came to your house this evening are spies of the Israelites sent to reconnoitre the whole country". He planned for the Israelites to be taken immediately to the palace, where they would be tortured until they confessed.

Now Rahab had heard of Yahweh, the God of the Israelites. Deep in her heart she had a longing to know this God, to leave her old life behind and follow his ways. As the king's messenger approached her house, she looked out and guessed immediately his business. Going in to where Joshua's men were already eating, she called out, "Quickly, you must hide. The king's guard is coming to arrest you". With great speed she led the men up to the flat roof of her house and covered them over with bundles of flax, which were drying in the sun before being woven into linen. "Lie there quietly," she commanded. "Do not stir, and above all, utter not even a whisper. When the messenger departs I will come and get you."

Hastening down the steps, Rahab was able to open the door to the king's messenger even as his fists beat a demand that he be admitted. Although the guard questioned and even threatened her, Rahab insisted that the men had come and gone. "I cannot say who they are or where they came from. They came seeking my favours and I turned them away. Go quickly now and you may well overtake them, for before the city gate was closed for the night they slipped away, although I know not where they went."

As soon as the guard had departed, Rahab locked her door and slipped up to where the spies were hidden on the roof. She called to them in a low voice to come out. Then she took them down into the house and explained why she had saved them. "I knew you to be Israelites as soon as I saw you," she told them. "I have heard about your Yahweh and I know in my heart that he will lead your army to victory and that the land of Canaan will be delivered up to you. I know, too, that your Yahweh is the Lord of both heaven and earth, for did he not drown the hosts of Pharaoh as they followed you through the waters of the Red Sea? I tell you, the king and his captains are in great fear, as are all the people. I, too, am afraid, but I am a woman who, although I have sinned much, would like to put my trust in Yahweh. So let me make a bargain with you. I have shown you kindness. Now, I beseech you show kindness to me and those I love. I would that I and my mother and my father and all my clansmen should be saved when your armies destroy this city, as they certainly will. I have kept faith with you. Pray you, keep faith with me."

The two spies answered her, "Our task is now accomplished. You have surely earned our gratitude. It shall be as you say. If we do not keep faith with you then it is we who deserve to die. When Yahweh delivers this city into our leader's hands we shall deal kindly with you and yours."

Then Rahab led Joshua's men to a window that hung out over the city wall. "Look you, now," she told them. "Here is a cord of scarlet, strongly woven. Let us fasten it firmly to the beam of the window; then you can escape down the wall. You must make quickly for the hills and hide there for three days to escape your pursuers. When the hunt is off you will be free to make your way back to the camp. Now, go quickly."

The two spies looked straight at the beautiful woman standing before them. "We thank you for what you have done, and for your trust. Now we swear by our God that you and your family will escape on the day of our coming. When we depart you must go secretly to your people and warn them that the assault will be soon. They must assemble in your house, every one of them, bound by oath not to tell anyone else what is happening. On the day of the assault you must give us a sign. Tie this scarlet cord to the window just as you have now done, and when our armies see it they will know that it shelters you, and you will be preserved. This we promise in the name of the God of all Israel. All within your door shall be safe, but if anyone ventures forth on that day we shall not be responsible for the blood that will flow."

Rahab vowed solemnly that all would be done as the spies said. Then she let them down by the cord to the foot of the city wall, and they were free to make their way by cover of night to the mountains.

For three days the Israelite men lay close, venturing forth only after dark for

food. Then on the third night they crossed the Jordan by a ford and returned to the camp of Joshua and reported to him all that had taken place. "Yahweh has delivered the entire land of Canaan into your hands," they told him. "Its inhabitants already tremble at the thought of our coming." Then they informed Joshua how Rahab had dealt with them and the promises they had made her, and Joshua assured them that it would all be as they had said.

On the very next day Joshua led the hosts of Israel towards the Jordan and they pitched their tents on the eastern shore. It was that time of the year when the Jordan is in flood, and the waters stretched before them for miles like an inland sea. For three days the Israelites camped, looking out over the swollen river, until Joshua gave the command to break camp and advance, with the priests bearing the sacred Ark of the Covenant at the head of the column.

Even as the feet of the priests bearing the Ark dipped into the edge of the water, a miracle occurred. The river, which until then had been running swiftly, was now dammed by debris about twenty miles upstream, and the Israelites were able to pass safely across. The army then marched toward Jericho, but camped at a place called Gilgal for many days to gather strength and practise the rites of their religion. On the fourteenth day of the first month of the new year they kept the feast of the Passover in celebration of their delivery out of Egypt.

Then the time came for Joshua to sound the command to advance. At last the battlements and towers of the great city of Jericho loomed into view.

In the shadow of the city wall Joshua looked up and saw a man standing before him, holding an unsheathed sword. As Joshua approached, the man's voice called, "I am the captain of the host of Yahweh come to meet you." As Joshua fell on his face before the figure the voice continued, "Take your sandals from off your feet, for you stand on holy ground". And Joshua did so.

Now Jericho was barricaded against the Israelites. No one came and no one went. Rahab had spoken truly. The king of Jericho and all the people feared greatly and trembled at the thought of the power of Yahweh.

The captain of Yahweh now spoke to Joshua. "Jericho and its king shall be delivered into your hands. Your warriors and fighting men must march once around the city every day for six days. On the seventh day they must march seven times around the town and the priests must blow their trumpets. When the trumpets sound, all your people must utter a fearsome war cry, shouting together with a mighty shout. When the trumpets and the shouting cease the walls of the city will come tumbling down and you will be able to storm the town and enter it."

Joshua did as he was bid. He summoned the priests to form a vanguard bearing the Ark of Yahweh and blowing on their ram's-horn trumpets while the army marched silently around the city. At daybreak for six days the host performed this awesome ritual while the king and captains of Jericho and the defenders of the city gazed in fearful wonder at the spectacle.

On the seventh day it happened as had been foretold. At the seventh time around the city the people shouted, the trumpets rang out and the walls of the city crumbled, then began to collapse. At once the people stormed the city until the entire town had been razed.

Only Rahab's house was spared. The two men who had been sent as spies did as Joshua commanded. Before the final sacking they saw Rahab's scarlet cord hanging as a sign. Quickly they entered the house and led out Rahab, her mother and father and all her clansmen, and took them swiftly to the safety of the Israelites' camp. Then all within the city were destroyed, except for the family of Rahab who were saved according to the pact made between Rahab and the spies of Joshua.

Legend has it that Rahab embraced the God of Israel, married Joshua, and was the ancestor of eight prophets and Huldah, the prophetess. She is included in the ancestry of Jesus and quoted in the New Testament of the bible as being a heroine of faith and justified by her deeds.

Esther: The Champion of Her People

The empire of King Ahasuerus the Persian was immense, stretching from India to Ethiopia. The king owned vast treasures and ruled over more than one hundred provinces. His slaves came from many nations, and in the capital of Susa there lived Jewish exiles from Canaan, captives whom Nebuchadnezzar, king of Babylon, had deported from Jerusalem.

In the third year of his reign, Ahasuerus gave a great banquet for all his princes and servants, his administrators, the chiefs of the army of Persia and Media, the nobles and the governors of his provinces. The celebration, which was the grandest ever known, went on for one hundred and eighty days.

For seven days afterwards the festivities continued for all the people of the city, from the highest to the lowest. The palace was draped with gorgeous hangings, couches decorated with precious stones were laid out on the marble pavements, and drinking was from golden cups, beautifully designed.

Queen Vashti also gave a banquet for all the women of the royal household, and there was much merry-making throughout Susa.

On the seventh day, when the king, who was flushed with wine, summoned Vashti to him, she refused to attend, and grievously offended her husband. Believing that he had lost face, he took the crown from her and banished her from his presence. Then he appointed commissioners to search out the most beautiful girls in the land so that he could take a new queen.

His choice fell upon Esther, who, although the king did not know it, was Jewish. She was an orphan and had been living with her guardian, Mordecai, and was extremely beautiful. She was also modest and simple, and soon won the admiration of everyone who saw her. She pleased the king so greatly that he set the royal diadem upon her head, proclaimed her queen and ordered another banquet, called Esther's banquet. A holiday was called throughout all the provinces.

Mordecai at this time was a servant at the palace chancellory, and it happened on a certain day that as he sat near the king's gate he overheard two malcontents whispering together and plotting to kill King Ahasuerus.

So he told Esther, and she told the king, and the two conspirators were caught and hanged. Yet the king and everyone else forgot to thank Mordecai or give him a reward for saving the king's life.

About this time the king was making a great favourite of an Amalekite who was called Haman. He raised his status so high that all the officials and servants of the chancellory were to bow down low and make obeisance when he passed by.

Only Mordecai remained upright, standing straight, refusing to prostrate himself as Haman went past, for he was of the race of Israel, a Jew, and the Israelites had been sworn enemies of the Amalekites from the time that they had come out of the land of Egypt. The officials of the chancellory were intrigued and continually asked Mordecai why he would not bow to Haman, but he gave them no reason. When Haman himself noticed Mordecai's behaviour, knowing that he was a Jew, he was very angry indeed and made up his mind to get rid of all Jews in the empire of Ahasuerus.

Haman waited his chance, and when the time was right he filled the King's ear with stories about the Jews, who, he said, had their own laws and refused to obey royal edicts. He even offered the king ten thousand talents of silver if he would order the Jews to be exterminated.

The king was so fond of Haman that he actually agreed, and told him to keep his money. What is more, he gave his signet ring to Haman, and told him that he might write any orders he liked, and seal them with the ring in the king's name.

So Haman wrote the letters ordering the massacre of the Jews and had them signed in the king's name and carried by fast runners to the governors of all the provinces of his empire. Ahasuerus and especially Haman were well enough pleased, but there was consternation in Susa and throughout the empire.

When Mordecai read the terrible proclamation, he guessed that Haman was really aiming at him, and he was dismayed that because of him thousands of innocent men, women and children were to be slain.

So he tore his clothes and put on sackcloth, covered his head with ashes, and went out into the streets, crying with a loud and bitter cry as far as the entry of the chancellory, which no one clothed in sackcloth was permitted to enter.

Throughout the empire Jews wept and fasted and prayed to Yahweh for deliverance.

When Esther's maids and chamberlain told her something of the news, she was deeply troubled, and sent clothes to her guardian, telling him to put off his sackcloth. But Mordecai refused. Instead, he sent to Esther, through a special messenger, a copy of the edict and a report of the money that Haman had been prepared to pay for the destruction of the Jews. He implored Esther to go to the king and plead with him to spare the people.

At first Esther replied that if she went to the king without being summoned, as was the custom at the court, she might well pay the penalty of death. In answer to that, Mordecai reminded her that she was also a Jewess, and would not be any safer than the rest of her race. "If you persist in remaining silent both you and your people will perish," he insisted. "Perhaps you have been made queen for the very purpose of saving your people."

Esther then sent this reply to Mordecai: "Go, gather together all the Jews who are living in Susa. Fast for me for three days and three nights, and I and my maids shall do the same. After that I will break the law and go into the king; and if I perish, I perish."

On the third day, Esther dressed herself sumptuously in her royal apparel and ventured into the forbidden ground of the king's court. Although she tried to appear calm she was inwardly trembling.

The king was sitting on his throne, and when he saw Esther looking so pale but lovely, he smiled and raising his golden sceptre he pointed toward her. Esther felt a great calm descend upon her. This was a sign that she was safe. So she drew nearer and touched the top of the sceptre. Then the king said to her, "What is the matter? Tell me what you desire and I will grant it, even if it is half my kingdom."

"What do I desire and what is my request?" replied Esther. "Only that you should honour me by coming with Haman to a banquet that I have prepared."

"Tell Haman to come at once", ordered the king, smiling. "Then Queen Esther can have her wish."

So the king and Haman came to the banquet and while they were drinking wine the king looked shrewdly at Esther, "Tell me what is on your mind. What is it that you want?"

"Only that you and Haman come tomorrow to another banquet that I have ordered," replied the queen. And the king agreed.

Haman was filled with pride and high spirits at the queen's behaviour toward him, but when he saw Mordecai at the chancellory still refusing to make obeisance before him he became bitterly angry. Rushing home he told his wife how the queen had honoured him. He sent for his friends and boasted of his glory and his exalted position. "But what do I care about all this," he said with a

71

frown, "when I see Mordecai, the Jew, sitting in the chancellory and refusing to stand up and bow?"

"Have a very high gallows erected," suggested his wife, "and ask the king's leave at the banquet to have Mordecai hanged upon it."

"And," added his friends, "you can then enjoy the banquet."

Delighted with this piece of advice, Haman had the gallows erected.

As things happened, that night the king could not sleep. As one of his servants was reading to him from the court chronicles, he came across the account of how Mordecai had once saved the king's life.

The king was deeply interested and a little troubled, and he asked, "What honour and dignity was conferred on Mordecai for this?"

"There was nothing done for him," was the reply.

"Who is on duty in the antechamber?" asked the king.

Now Haman was so eager to have Mordecai hanged that he had not been able to wait until the next day at the banquet, but had come that night to ask the king's permission for the hanging, and he was in the antechamber.

Ahasuerus was pleased to see his favourite and he consulted with him, "What should I do to a man whom I wish to honour?"

Haman thought to himself, "That man, of course, can only be me." So he answered the King: "Let the royal clothing that the king has worn be brought, and the horse which the king has ridden on, with the royal diadem on its head. Let this clothing and the horse be delivered to one of the king's most noble officers. Let that officer go to the man the king wishes to honour, put upon him the royal clothing, and bring him back on horseback through the streets of the city, proclaiming before him, 'This is the way the king treats the one whom he wishes to honour.'"

The king was delighted with the answer.

"Hurry and take the clothing and the horse as you have just said to Mordecai, the Jew, at the chancellory. Array him royally, and let it be just as you described."

Haman dared not disobey. He was the "most noble officer", and he must do as the king commanded.

So he took the robes and the horse and arrayed Mordecai and led him back through the streets proclaiming, "This is the way the king treats the one whom he wishes to honour."

Afterwards Mordecai returned to the chancellory and Haman hurried home dejected and full of woe. His wife was of little comfort. As they were talking, the king's eunuchs arrived to escort Haman to Queen Esther's banquet.

As they were again drinking wine, toward the end of the banquet, the king turned once more to Esther, "Tell me in truth what is on your mind. Tell me what you desire and I will grant it, even if it is half my kingdom."

"If I have pleased you as a wife, O king," replied Queen Esther, "and if it please your majesty, allow me my life. That is my desire; and my request is that you spare the lives of my people, for we have been sold to destruction and extermination. The order has been given."

"Who is the man who would make such an order?" asked the king. In his heart he was astonished for he knew not that the queen was a Jewess and he had forgotten about the signet ring. "Who is your persecutor?"

Esther replied, turning toward Haman, "The man? The persecutor? Why, this wretched Haman. He is the one who has ordered the destruction of the Jews — me and my people."

Haman fell back in terror, and the king, in a rage, left the banquet and went out to the palace garden to control his thoughts.

Then Haman flung himself at the queen and began to beg for his life. When the king came in from the garden he found Haman huddled over the couch on which Esther was lying. "What now! Is he going to attack her before my eyes and in my own palace?" he raged.

One of the king's eunuchs who was in attendance looked at the king and shrugged. "It is very convenient: just outside the palace there is a gallows which this fellow Haman had erected for Mordecai, the man who saved the king's life."

"Then hang the wretched man on it at once," cried the king in anger. And they carried Haman out and hanged him.

That day the king gave Esther the house and property of Haman, and Mordecai was presented formally to the king as Queen Esther's guardian. The king, who had recovered his signet ring, once more took it off, and gave it to Mordecai, and Esther put Mordecai in charge of her household.

Once more Esther defied the conventions of the court and petitioned the king to have revoked the edict Haman had issued in the king's name. "How can I look on and see my people suffer? How can I bear to witness their extermination?" she asked.

"Do not worry," said the king. "Mordecai is free to write as he thinks fit, and seal it with my ring, for any order written in the King's name and sealed with his signet is binding."

The royal scribes were summoned in haste and Mordecai dictated an order granting the Jews freedom from arrest and persecution which he wrote in the name of Ahasuerus and which he sealed with the king's signet. These letters were carried by courier throughout the length and breadth of the empire and Queen Esther was known far and wide as the champion of her people.

Judith and Holofernes

Nebuchadnezzar, king of Ninevah, was furious with those countries, including Judaea, which had refused to join his war against the king of the Medes. After routing the entire army of the Medes, Nebuchadnezzar planned his revenge on the countries that had not supported his campaign. He summoned Holofernes, the commander-in-chief of his armies, second only to himself in power, and ordered him to go on a rampage of retaliation. "Go," he said, "begin with the regions close by, and then spread out. If the people of a region surrender to you, spare their lives, but if they oppose you, show no mercy. Put them to the sword and plunder their territory. Now go, and do as I command!"

Holofernes at once gathered his generals and chiefs of staff and handpicked a hundred and twenty thousand troops, along with twelve thousand mounted bowmen, whom he organized into battle formation. The army was well equipped and generously rationed. It appeared invincible.

So it proved. The army cut its way through vast territories, over mountain ranges and across deserts, burning and pillaging as it went. Entire wheat harvests were destroyed, fields fired, flocks and herds wiped out, towns sacked, temples plundered, and the countryside laid waste. The young men of the regions were all slaughtered.

When news of this holocaust reached the Israelites living in Judaea they were greatly alarmed. In former years their holy city of Jerusalem had been sacked and the Jews had been returned from captivity for only a short time. The people had only just resettled in Judaea and their Temple to Yahweh, which had been profaned, had not long been reconsecrated.

Now as they heard of the approaching army, they fasted, draped their altar in sackcloth and wore sackcloth themselves, covered their heads with ashes, and begged the God of Israel not to allow their little ones to be carried off, their wives slaughtered and their heritage destroyed. Then they prepared to do battle with the army of Holofernes by closing the mountain passes, fortifying the summits and putting down traps on the plains.

Holofernes was incensed, and ordered Achior, the commander of the Ammonites, in whose territory he was now camped, to tell him what he knew of these resistant mountain people. So Achior told Holofernes how the sons of Israel had settled in Canaan, how they had migrated to Egypt in a time of famine, where they had been enslaved, how they had been delivered from Egypt, wandered through the desert and had finally returned to Canaan, driving out all the inhabitants of the region. He told Holofernes, too, that while the sons of Israel lived lives pleasing to their God they were protected from their enemies, but how when they departed from the ways of behaviour commanded by their God they were slain in battle and many were taken captive to foreign lands. Achior advised Holofernes not to attack before he had discovered whether or not the people had sinned and offended their God. "For if they are guiltless people," he said, "then God will protect them, and any attacker might end up being the laughing-stock of the entire world."

This made Holofernes even angrier, and his men began to urge him to attack the Israelites, a weak and powerless people, after all. But his anger was directed especially at Achior, who dared to speak up for the Israelites. So Holofernes commanded his orderlies to hand him over to the enemy, but as the party approached the town of Bethulia they were pelted with stones from the catapults of the Israelites. So they left Achior bound at the foot of the mountain on which the town was built, and retreated.

The Israelites then came down from the town and carried Achior away for questioning. Achior told the Israelites that Holofernes was openly boasting about what he would do to the Jewish people.

Indeed, the very next day Holofernes marched on Bethulia, occupying the mountain passes and placing the town under siege. An army of one hundred and twenty thousand infantrymen and twelve thousand cavalrymen paraded before the town, striking fear into the hearts of the Israelites. The next day Holofernes reconnoitred the approaches to the mountain town and placed guards at all the water springs to cut off the town's water supply. He intended to starve the Israelites before attacking. They would pay dearly for their defiance.

And they did. After thirty-four days every water jar in Bethulia was dry, the wells were nigh exhausted, and even with water-rationing there was not enough water to quench the thirst of the people. Food supplies were also running out and the people, especially the very young and the aged, were beginning to collapse from sheer exhaustion and malnutrition.

Each day the elders of the city gathered in council, but although they prayed and tried to put their trust in Yahweh, their hearts were failing them with fear.

There came the point when they felt they could hold out no longer. Uzziah, the chief elder of the town, made a hard decision. "Elders of Bethulia," he said, "be strong. Let us hold out for five days longer. In that time our God, Yahweh, will show us the way and send deliverance to his people, so be of good cheer." In spite of Uzziah's brave words the elders were dispirited, and a gloom spread through the town like a plague.

Now in Bethulia there lived a very wealthy widow called Judith, the daughter of a Jew descended directly from Israel, and a woman of stunning beauty as well as great importance. Her husband, Manasseh, an important man in his own right, had died of sunstroke at the time of the barley harvest four years previously. In all that time Judith had lived modestly as a widow. She had an upper room built for her on the roof of her house, where she lived simply and frugally, wearing widow's weeds and an apron of sackcloth. She fasted frequently except for the Sabbath eve and the Sabbath day and for festivals such as that of the New Moon and those kept by the House of Israel. Although she had vast possessions and numerous servants, both male and female, her simplicity of life, her devout behaviour and her gentle disposition made her loved by all who knew her. Yet underneath her modest appearance lay great strength of mind and an heroic spirit.

When Judith heard of Uzziah's decision to surrender in five days unless a miracle occurred, observing the faint hearts of the hungry and thirst-ridden people, she summoned the town elders to her house and met them in the upper room.

"Listen to me," she said, "it was very wrong of Uzziah to utter such a pronouncement and for your elders to take an oath to surrender the town in five days if our God failed us. Can't you see that you are daring to put Yahweh to a test? That is very wrong. If you don't understand the mind of your fellow man how can you presume to know the mind of the Almighty God? You really understand very little, and you never will! You have no right to demand guarantees of help and favour from our God. He will help us if he sees fit.

"But can't you have faith? Our God has never deserted us when we have fully honoured him. Rather, he has always been good to us. If we give in to Holofernes and his army it is not only the people of Bethulia who will suffer. The whole of Judaea will be sacked and our holy places profaned. As a nation we will be shamed, and we will be a disgrace to Yahweh.

"If you agree with what I say, let us give praise to our God, who is testing us at this time."

To this speech Uzziah replied quite simply, "Everything you say is true, Judith. No one would deny a word you have uttered. But you can see for yourself that people are dying of thirst, and their very plight has forced us into the situation of making a decision which we ourselves find abhorrent. You are a good

and devout woman. So you pray to the Almighty to send rain to fill our wells and our water troughs so that we might have the strength to resist the enemy."

Judith looked hard at Uzziah. "Listen well," she said, "we have been given minds to use and I have a plan; and I intend to carry it out. The memory of what I am going to do will be passed down through history. Tonight I and my attendant will come to the gate of Bethulia. You must be there, and do not ask me what I am going to do. But this I tell you. Before the five days you have decreed have passed I shall have rescued Israel from our enemies. I promise you."

All Uzziah and the chiefs could say was, "We trust you. Go in peace and may the Lord be with you."

As soon as the elders had left her alone Judith scattered ashes over her head and prayed long to her God, asking him to give her strength in her undertaking; for she knew in her heart exactly what she must do.

After her impassioned prayer Judith called her attendant and went down into the main body of the house, which she normally visited only on the Sabbath and feast days. With the help of her attendant she removed her sackcloth and her widow's weeds, bathed her body and perfumed herself, then dressed in her most elaborate robes, the best that she had ever worn when she and her husband had attended important banquets. Her hair was elaborately coiled and twined with precious stones, gems sparkled at her ears and she adorned herself with bracelets, rings and all her glittering jewellery. Even her sandals were elaborately worked. She made a breathtaking sight.

Then Judith and her attendant gathered the best provisions left in the house; a skin of wine, a flask of oil, loaves of bread and girdle cakes, figs, raisins and olives. These were all wrapped and placed in a bag. Quickly they left the house and made their way to the gate of the town.

Uzziah and the chiefs were amazed at the change in Judith, and struck by her radiance, but made no comment except to bless her in the name of the god of Israel. Then they opened the gate and Judith and her attendant went outside, picked their way down the mountainside until they were lost from sight in the valley.

It wasn't long before Judith and her attendant were accosted by an advance guard from Holofernes' army, who immediately began firing questions at Judith. The soldiers looked with amazement at the sight of such a beautiful and splendidly arrayed woman out in the countryside with only one attendant. Who was she? From whence did she come? What was her business?

To their questions Judith replied that she was a Hebrew woman who was running away from Bethulia because she knew that it would soon be occupied by Holofernes, whom she was now seeking. "I could show him how to capture the town without losing a single soldier," she promised.

"Well, that indeed may save your life," said the captain, "seeing that you have taken the initiative. We will lead you to the tent of Holofernes immediately. When you meet him, don't be afraid. Just tell him all that you have told us, and all will be well."

With an escort of one hundred men, Judith was taken to the camp headquarters and to the tent of the commander. The news of this beautiful Hebrew woman, discovered out in the valley, spread like wildfire through the camp. Soldiers came running from their tents to stare in wonder at her beauty. They stood in little groups lost in admiration while Judith waited to be taken in to Holofernes.

Inside his tent Holofernes was stretched out on a bed hung with a purple and gold canopy, which was studded with gemstones. Soldiers carrying silver flares led Judith forward. As the light illuminated the stunning vision of the graceful figure and finely wrought features of Judith arrayed like a princess, Holofernes started up with astonishment. Even as Judith bowed low in homage before him he signed to his servants to lift her up. He couldn't keep his eyes from her face or her figure.

"Never fear, woman," he said softly, "I shall see to it that no harm is done to you, for you have come to us. But, tell me, why have you done so?"

Judith spoke flatteringly to Holofernes. "You are in the service of the great king Nebuchadnezzar, and because of your command even the birds of the air and the cattle, the oxen, the asses and the sheep live for service to the king. You, his chief commander, are known throughout the world for your intelligence and your genius in war. There is no other commander in the world like you."

Then Judith told how Achior had been taken into the city by the men of Bethulia and had reported what he had told Holofernes about the Jews. "It is true, my lord, as Achior has spoken. And because the Israelites have done wrong and offended their God you will overcome them. They are now starving, and they have run out of water, so they are coming to the point where they will be prepared to eat the food set aside for the Temple. That would be a great sin and Yahweh would punish the Jews by allowing you to conquer them. That is why I have come to you. I am a devoted Jew, and I shall go with my attendant each night out into the valley to pray. When I know that the people of Bethulia have committed this sin I will come to you and you will know that it is the time to attack."

Holofernes was gleeful. "You are as wise as you are beautiful and as beautiful as you are eloquent," he told Judith. "You did well to come to me. I shall see that you make your home in the palace of King Nebuchadnezzar, and your fame shall spread throughout our world. Do as you promise and I shall adopt your god as my god, and take you to the king myself."

Holofernes then led Judith in to where his table was set with silver and would have sat her down to table with him, but Judith murmured, "That would not be right, my lord, I have brought my own food and drink. It is better this way."

"As you wish," replied Holofernes.

After they had eaten, an adjutant took Judith to a tent and there she slept until midnight. Just before dawn she went out to the valley to pray as she had arranged with Holofernes. But first she purified herself at a spring of water which was guarded by pickets, then after prayer she returned to her tent. This procedure she followed for three nights.

On the fourth day of her stay in the camp Holofernes ordered a banquet to be prepared at which the choicest of foods were to be served on a silver service, and where rare wine would be poured from silver jugs into finely wrought goblets. His chamberlain was sent to invite Judith to the feast.

Carefully Judith decked herself out in her finest array. "Should I deny my lord his pleasure?" was the message that she sent, and the heart of Holofernes leapt with desire for the Hebrew woman. When she appeared to take her place at the banquet he could not take his eyes from her, and he wanted desperately to embrace her.

A special woolly fleece was laid out for her to lie on as she ate. "Drink up," commanded Holofernes, "eat with us and enjoy yourself."

"Never have I been so greatly honoured, my lord," replied Judith, "I shall always remember this day."

Judith reclined opposite Holofernes and gazed across at him as she ate, but she ate only of the provisions which she and her attendant had prepared and brought with them.

As for Holofernes, he was enchanted. The beauty of Judith flushed his head like wine and the wine in his goblet was replenished again and again until his senses and his whole body reeled. The night wore on, and Holofernes was too drunk to move. His servants cleared away the remains of the banquet and set out his bed before going off duty, leaving only Judith and her attendant in the tent with Holofernes. Already Holofernes was in a drunken slumber.

Judith told her attendant to wait outside. Midnight had passed and, as she was wont to do, Judith would shortly be going out to the valley to wash and to pray. The guards were well used to the ritual.

When Judith was alone in the tent with Holofernes she went to the bedpost by the commander's head and took hold of his broad, curved sword which hung there. Bracing herself she cried to her God for strength of body and spirit. Then grasping Holofernes by the hair she raised his head and smote with the sword so that the head was severed from the body. Quickly she pulled the canopy from the bed and wrapped it around the body. The head she placed in her food bag and covered it with a cloth. This she gave to her attendant who was waiting outside the tent, and together the two women left the camp, as they did each night, to pray. Outside the camp they edged around the ravine and climbed the mountainside to the gate of Bethulia.

As she approached the gate Judith shouted to the guard, "Open the gate! God has not deserted us!" As soon as she was inside the walls of the city the elders and the people, down to the children, came running and surrounded her.

There she stood, her beauty shining like a flame of living fire. "Praise to the God of Israel!" she shouted as she drew out the severed head of Holofernes from her bag. "Here is the head of Holofernes, commander of the army of Nebuchad-nezzar; and here is the canopy from the bed where he fell down drunk. He has been struck down by the hand of a woman and with his own sword. Glory be to God."

The townspeople, overcome with joyful emotion, fell on their knees and gave thanks to their God. Uzziah turned to Judith and blessed her, "Your strength of mind shall be remembered forever among the heroes of Israel". And the people shouted, "Amen! Amen!"

As day broke, dispersing the shadows of night, the soldiers of the town hung the head of Holofernes from the ramparts. At Judith's bidding, the Jews streamed down the mountainside and attacked the camp of Holofernes. When the sentries heard them coming they rushed to the commander's tent, where they discovered his headless body. Consternation and turmoil gathered force in the camp. They had all been duped by the Hebrew woman, and now an army was descending on them like a pack of raging wolves. Panic broke out. Before the captains could rally the cavalry the Israelites were upon them. The army was annihilated.

For thirty days the Jews looted the camp. They gave to Judith the tent of Holofernes with his silver plate, bowls and goblets, his finery and his furniture. All these things she loaded on to a pack of mules. Then she led a procession of women, wearing garlands of olive leaves, waving branches, singing and dancing, as they climbed back up the mountain side to Bethulia before setting out for Jerusalem, the holy city.

There, the company from Bethulia were purified in the Temple before offering their booty to be shared with the people. The rejoicing and thanksgiving lasted for three months. Then they all returned home to Bethulia.

In her home town Judith lived to a gracious old age managing her estates. Her fame spread even beyond Israel and men came from many lands to woo her. But although she set aside her sackcloth and her widow's weeds, she refused all her suitors. When she died she was over one hundred years old, much loved and greatly revered. Her possessions were shared among her family and that of her husband Manasseh. Her body was buried in the cave by the side of her husband, and the people mourned her passing for seven days. But her memory lives on in their hearts.

Bilqĩs:
The Queen of Sheba

The story of the visit of the queen of Sheba to King Solomon in the tenth century BC, as told in the Old Testament, has inspired poets and painters through the ages. In both Jewish and Islamic tradition the queen referred to was Bilqĩs, ruler of the kingdom of Saba (or Sheba) in southwestern Arabia. In Ethiopian literature she is known as Makeda. Her story is told in the Qur'ân (or Koran), though she is not mentioned by name. She is the subject of a widespread cycle of Arab legends, and her story also appears in Persian literature, in which she is considered to be the daughter of a Chinese emperor. According to Ethiopian tradition, Makeda married Solomon. Their son, Menelik I, is considered to be the founder of the royal dynasty of Ethiopia.

In the Old Testament and other Jewish writings the queen of Saba visited Solomon at the head of a camel caravan, bearing gold, jewels and spices. The purpose of her visit was to test the king's wisdom by asking him a series of riddles.

Saba lay along the route to the Indian Ocean and was rich in gold, frankincense and myrrh. Solomon needed the products of Saba for maintaining his commercial enterprises, and the queen needed Solomon's co-operation in marketing her goods in the Mediterranean and his Palestinian ports.

From whatever sources her story is taken, the queen of Sheba is an awe-inspiring figure, personifying the richness, opulence and elegance of a Middle Eastern potentate of twelve centuries ago — a woman who could hold her own with one of the greatest kings in Jewish history.

It was told long ago in the town bazaars and nomadic camps of Arabia that the beautiful young woman, Bilqĩs, was the offspring of the king of Saba, born after he married a daughter of the king of the jinn. (In Mohammedan lore the jinn (genies) were spirits a little lower than the angels, who were able to appear in human or animal form and had supernatural powers over mortals.)

The strange marriage had taken place after the king of Saba had been disturbed while hunting by two serpents locked in combat — one a deadly black, the other white. The king killed the black one, but allowed the white serpent to slither away free.

When he returned to his palace the king could not take his mind off his encounter with the serpents, and he was not surprised to receive, soon after, a visit from a tall man who suddenly appeared out of thin air in his chamber.

"Do not be afraid," said the apparition, "I am the white serpent whose life you spared. The black one you killed was my slave, who had rebelled against my authority. In return for your kindness to me in allowing me to live, I now bestow upon you great riches and the gift of healing."

Although the king was already wealthy beyond measure, he valued greatly the gift of healing and was so grateful that he asked the stranger whether he had a daughter, and, if so, he said, he would wish to marry her.

"Indeed you shall," affirmed the stranger, "but on the condition that whatever she may do you must never question her actions, no matter how strange they may seem to you."

So the king married the jinee princess and in due time a son was born to them. When he saw his wife throw the baby into the kitchen fire, the king was deeply upset and angry; but because of his promise to the jinee, he said nothing, but kept his counsel.

When a daughter was born and she was thrown to a huge, ferocious dog, who ran off with her in his mouth, the king was even more upset and even angrier; but because of his promise to the jinee, said nothing.

Time passed, and a rebellion broke out in the kingdom. The king, with the queen at his side, rode off to deal with the rebels. One night the king looked out beyond the camp fire to see all his supplies being rolled off the camels' backs by unseen hands, and the drinking water being emptied into the sand. The king could remain silent no longer. He rounded on his wife and accused her of murdering their children. Now she had summoned a band of invisible jinn to destroy him in the desert. What sort of a thing was she!

Sadly his wife explained to him that he should have trusted her completely. The provisions and water had been poisoned, she told the king, by a treacherous chief-councillor who had been bribed by the enemy. But, never fear, she would lead the king to a nearby well, where he could obtain fresh water, and to a place where there were new supplies.

As to the murder of their children, the boy had been given into the care of a nursemaid, but had unhappily fallen ill and died. Their daughter, Bilqīs, was not only safe, but radiantly alive.

Even as the queen was speaking, the earth by the king's feet shook, then split apart. Out of the fissure that opened before him stepped a dazzlingly beautiful

83

young woman with shining dark eyes and long, dark hair, which cascaded like a cloak about her. His daughter ran forward to embrace him, but the queen looked sadly into the king's face, then disappeared forever from his sight.

Bilqĩs grew up to be a talented and beautiful woman, much loved by her father and all who came into contact with her. When her father died she was deeply distressed, but even more so when her cousin, an evil, lecherous older man, was made king. Well she knew that no woman in the court was safe from his well-plotted advances. Act she must; otherwise, no woman in the kingdom of any beauty was safe.

Splendidly dressed, Bilqĩs visited the new king and offered herself to him in marriage. Nothing could suit the wretch better, so plans were made for a speedy wedding.

The ceremony took place with due pomp and ceremony, but with little rejoicing. The new queen's household servants, her attendants and the courtiers were plunged into a gloom so black that they took no delight at all in the feasting and dancing that followed the wedding ceremony.

Bilqĩs, however, remained lively and gay, quickly replenishing her husband's goblet well before he had drained it. That night, in their private chambers, she continued to ply him with wine, and when he was quite drunk she drew her sword, and beheaded him. Her Sabean subjects were overjoyed by her action. They proclaimed her sole ruler of the kingdom, and promised her loyalty and love.

To prove their devotion they built Bilqĩs a palace of onyx, marble and alabaster. Its golden domes towered to the sky. Underneath the central dome they erected a burnished throne, the like of which had never before been seen. Its canopy rose high into the air. On either side, huge golden branches intertwined to spread boughs, from which hung garlands of precious stones and jewelled flowers that shone like stars in a velvet sky. The rising sun was never more splendid than the throne from which Bilqĩs ruled the kingdom of Saba — or Sheba as it was known in the faraway land of Palestine, where King Solomon ruled, also in great splendour.

It is from the Qur'ân, as well as from the Old Testament, that we learn of the glory and majesty with which Solomon ruled. Because Solomon loved Yahweh and had chosen wisdom and understanding above riches, God had blessed him with both discernment and great wealth. Three times a year Solomon offered holocausts, or burnt-offerings, and communion sacrifices on the altar he had built for Yahweh.

Not only did Solomon rule over the people of his kingdom but the Qur'ân tells how he ruled the beasts of the field, the birds of the air, even the demons, spirits and spectres of the night. He knew the language of all creatures and they understood his.

When Solomon was cheered with wine, it was sometimes his custom to hold court with birds, beasts and lively creatures, both of the earth and of the spirit world. On one occasion, the hoopoe bird, with its distinctive plumage and tufted crest, was missing from the assembly. Solomon was angry and sent out a party to bring the hoopoe to him, immediately. As it was, the hoopoe was already approaching the king with an amazing story of what he had seen in Sheba. "A kingdom ruled by a woman," he exclaimed, "to whom everything has been given and who reigns from a magnificent throne. So rich is she that sand is more valuable than gold, and silver is like mud in the streets. The trees of the city are from the beginning of time, and they are nourished by water from the Garden of Eden.

"But the queen and her people worship the sun to the exclusion of God. Surely the king should invite this monarch to his court to convince her that God is great, and to be worshipped."

The words of the hoopoe pleased Solomon, whose clerks penned a letter at his command and tied it to the hoopoe's wing. The bird rose skyward and flew toward Sheba, followed by a host of the birds of the air.

In Sheba Queen Bilqīs had gone forth to worship the sun. Suddenly the arriving birds cast shadows across the slanting rays, and the hoopoe alighted by the queen, offering her the letter bound to his wing.

After reading the letter the queen summoned her princes and elders informing them that Solomon had invited her to visit him. "O my people," she said, "advise me how to decide!"

"It is for you to decide," they told her. "We know nought of this king but what is contained in the message from the bird."

"Then we will send this Solomon a most magnificent gift. If he is a worldly king he will accept it. If he is truly a messenger of God he will not accept it, but plead with us further to follow his God."

So Bilqīs assembled her sea-going ships and loaded them with wood, pearls and precious gems. As well she sent to Solomon six thousand youths and maidens, all born at the same hour, on the same day, in the same year, all of equal stature and size and clothed in purple. With them she sent a small glass bottle. Inside the bottle she had placed a large, unpierced pearl, and an emerald which had been unevenly pierced.

As she entrusted the bottle to one of her counsellors she said, "Watch this Solomon carefully. If he is cross and churlish he is no man of God. If he is kind and gentle, he is what he claims to be."

Solomon, surrounded by his own wise men and retinue, received Bilqīs's emissaries in the splendour of his court. He listened graciously to all that they had to say, but refused the queen's gifts, affirming politely that he had riches enough of his own. "God has given me the gift of wisdom. What more do I want?" he told them.

It was then that Bilqīs's counsellor produced the glass bottle, and asked Solomon to guess what it contained.

"Why, an unpierced pearl and an emerald unevenly pierced," stated Solomon.

"The queen would have you pierce the pearl and string the uneven emerald," the counsellor then told the king. "Can you do it?"

Solomon consulted with his wise men and magicians. Then he summoned a wood-turner who quickly pierced the pearl. He was gazing thoughtfully at the emerald when a tiny worm at his feet spoke up in a weak and reedy voice. "I can do it, O my lord." Taking a thread in its mouth the worm wriggled its way through the emerald to emerge on the other side with thread enough to string the jewel. Then Solomon returned the pearl and the emerald to the bottle, and sent it back, with the other gifts to Bilqīs.

When the long procession returned to the queen's palace in Sheba, and all that had happened and all that was said was reported to her, Bilqīs decided to visit Solomon herself. But before she set out on her journey she bade her servants hide her golden throne in a miniature palace, around which they were to build seven other palaces. The queen herself then locked the doors of each of the palaces and set guards outside them.

Slowly the glittering caravan of the queen of Sheba made its way to Jerusalem. There were camels laden with costly spices, vast quantities of gold and precious stones. Never had that city witnessed such a spectacular sight.

Solomon looked out with awe, and wondered how he could best show his appreciation of the splendour that had been assembled in his honour. It was the hoopoe bird who confided in Solomon how the queen had secured her throne before leaving Sheba.

Then Solomon said, "O my people! Which of you will transport the queen's throne to Jerusalem before the queen and her entourage arrive?"

One of the jinn said, "I will fetch it for you before you can stand up and sit down. That I can honestly do."

"No, I want it this instant," replied the king.

"Then I shall bring it to you in a twinkling of an eye," said the lord of the jinn.

"Then do so," said Solomon. "But disguise the throne. We will see if the queen will recognise it, for she will only do so if she is inspired of God." He said this because it was said that the people of Sheba worshipped idols to the exclusion of God, and were a nation of unbelievers.

Even as Solomon spoke, the solid earth around the king's own throne seemed to melt away, and the throne of Bilqis rose up as though through the surface of a lake to stand beside that of the king. Even Solomon was amazed, and his attendants gasped in amazement.

By now Bilqīs was about to enter the city. Solomon sent one of his most handsome officers, Benaiah, to meet her. It was said that Benaiah was as fair as the first flush in the eastern sky at the break of day. As the evening star outshines all other stars, so Benaiah outshone other men. He stood straight, like a lily growing by a brook.

When the queen caught sight of him she descended from her chariot to do him honour; but Benaiah rebuked her saying, "Do not let your feet touch the ground, O queen. It is I who must honour you!"

"Are you not King Solomon, then?" she demanded of him. Benaiah replied, "Not King Solomon, gracious lady, but one of his servants sent to welcome you on his behalf."

Then the queen turned to the nobles around her and said, "If you have not seen the lion, you have at least seen his lair. If you have not yet seen King Solomon you have at least seen the beauty of him who stands in his presence."

Benaiah then conducted the queen into the court of Solomon, who had commanded the jinn to build him a palace of green glassware with a courtyard paved with glass.

The glass had been made by magic to look like water, and under the glass there were set fishes and other aquatic creatures which gave the illusion of being alive in the sea.

This had been done by the demons and other creatures which inhabited Solomon's court and who had been talking among themselves. Secretly, they were afraid that when Solomon saw the queen's beauty he would want to marry her. Then should a son be born to the royal couple the demons, jinn and other creatures would be in bondage forever to the descendants of the king and queen. So the wily creatures told Solomon that Bilqīs, for all her outward beauty, had the legs of a donkey and that she was sick and of an unsound mind.

The tricksters then arranged for the queen to walk across the glass courtyard to approach the king's throne. As she stepped forward and saw the sea creatures apparently darting about her feet, the queen really thought that she had ventured into a lake of water, and lifted her skirts to prevent them from becoming wet.

Solomon, watching Bilqīs approach, was embarrassed to see upon her legs soft downy curls. Modestly turning his eyes away from this unexpected sight he hastened to reassure the queen. "It is only a glass paved court that looks like water. Do not be disconcerted, but come and join me here."

Quickly dropping the hem of her robe Bilqīs stepped forward, exclaiming; "My Lord, I have indeed behaved foolishly, but I now submit myself to Solomon, and to God, the lord of the universe."

Then indicating the throne that had been brought from Sheba by magic, Solomon asked the queen, "Is this your throne, fair queen?"

"It certainly looks like it," replied Bilqīs, hiding her surprise.

"Then, come sit upon it, here beside me," bade Solomon gently, for her

answer satisfied him that her mind was not only sound, but sharp. Had she denied the throne to be hers, or violently asserted her right to it, he would have suspected her judgement.

When the queen of Sheba had taken her place on her own throne beside Solomon, she turned to him and said; "Great things have I heard about the splendour of your person and the depth of your wisdom. The first I have seen for myself. Now, pray, my lord, answer me these riddles.

"What water belongs neither to heaven nor earth?" she asked.

"That I can answer readily," replied Solomon. "If my horses gallop until sweat streams down their flanks and legs and if I collect that sweat in basins, then I have water that belongs neither to heaven nor earth."

"Well then, what is it that living moves not, but when its head is cut off it moves?"

"It is a ship in the sea," replied Solomon.

Solomon had an answer for all of the queen's many riddles. Not one of them was too obscure for the king to explain.

Then, to test him further, Bilqīs ordered a number of men and women, all of the same stature and all dressed alike, to stand in a line before Solomon. "Distinguish the men from the women," she commanded him.

Solomon immediately signed to his eunuchs standing by, who brought in a silver platter of nuts and roasted ears of corn, which they then offered to the waiting line of people. The men, unabashed, seized the nuts and corn with their bare hands; but the women took them daintily in gloved hands, extended from beneath their garments. Then Solomon called out triumphantly, "Those are the men, and these the women."

After Bilqīs, queen of Sheba, had put Solomon to the test and had seen with her own eyes the splendour of his palace, the magnificent accommodation for his officials, the efficient organisation of his staff, the rich robes of his cup-bearers, the abundance and quality of the fare served at his table and the sacrifices which he offered in the Temple of Yahweh, she was breathless with amazement.

She said to Solomon, "Everything I heard in my own country about you and your wisdom is true, then! Until I came and saw with my own eyes I could not believe what I heard. Now I see that I was told less than half, for your wisdom and prosperity surpass everything I have ever been told about you. Blessed be Yahweh, your God, who has granted you his favour, and set you upon the throne of Israel."

The queen then presented Solomon with one hundred and twenty talents of gold, along with vast quantities of spices and precious stones. Never had there been known such an array of spices as the queen of Sheba presented to King Solomon. The queen's fleet, which carried gold from Ophir, brought to Solomon great cargoes of sandalwood, which the king used in making columns for the Temple of Yahweh and for his royal palace, and for harps and lyres for the royal musicians.

King Solomon, in his turn, presented the queen of Sheba with many gifts from his royal treasure house and with everything that she admired. Then she returned home, with her servants and retinue, to her own country.

Ethiopian legend has it that Solomon did marry the queen of Sheba. Before the wedding ceremony the jinn removed the hairs on the queen's legs by applying a depilatory ointment made from lime — the first example in human history of such cosmetic treatment.

Jewish legend and the Bible story insist that the queen returned directly to Sheba after having proclaimed her faith in God.

Arabic sources say that on her return to Saba the queen married a neighbouring king with whom she had long been friendly. They then ruled their two kingdoms jointly, supported by Solomon's jinn, who helped them build many fortresses and palaces and who served the queen faithfully until the death of Solomon, or Sulayman, as he was known in the Arabic.

Scheherazade

The Arabian Nights' Entertainments, or the Thousand and One Nights, is a collection of popular tales from Arabia, parts of the Middle East and India. The stories span many centuries and include Aladdin, Ali Baba, and Sinbad the Sailor. They were well known in Europe in the eighteenth century.

The collection was published in France between 1704 and 1717 as *Mille et une nuits* by Antoine Galland, who based his version on a Syrian manuscript, but added tales from other sources.

The framing story is that of Scheherazade, but she enters the narrative only after an elaborate account of a sultan's betrayal, which explains his cruelty and callousness. It came about thus.

The Sassanians, who were the ancient kings of Persia, ruled for about four hundred years. Their territories extended from Persia to beyond the Ganges, as far as China. One of the most illustrious of the Persian kings had two sons, Schahriar, the elder, and Schahzaman.

When the king died, Schahriar inherited the entire kingdom, but so great was his affection for his brother that he divided his realm and gave the country of Great Tartary to Schahzaman to rule over it. Schahzaman made Samarkand the capital and seat of government and took up residence there, where he married a beautiful woman in whom his heart delighted.

After a period of years Schahriar sent his Grand Vizier to Samarkand, inviting Schahzaman to visit him at the capital of the Indes. Schahzaman was delighted and made preparations to leave at once for the capital. On the day of his departure he bade his wife a fond farewell, and with his Vizier rode out from the city, shortly pitching his tent for the night. Alone in his tent, desire for his wife overcame the prince. Saddling a horse he returned at midnight to the palace and

91

went at once to the princess's apartments. Thinking to surprise his wife, he stole silently to her chamber, only to behold her, by the light of his flambeau, sharing a goblet of wine and in amorous embrace with one of his officers. In a fury the prince drew his scimitar and dispatched his wife and the officer with a single blow. He then proceeded to the capital of the Indes to visit his brother, the sultan Schahriar.

Throughout the visit, no matter what entertainment the sultan arranged, Schahzaman found it impossible to free his mind of the memory of his unfaithful wife. Instead of entering into the hunting-matches and musical amusements arranged for him, Schahzaman preferred to walk alone in the palace gardens, brooding on his wife's betrayal.

One day when he was thus walking, he heard the tinkling of laughter as a party of women, including the sultana, his brother's wife, trailed through the groves of the garden. Not wishing to be observed, Schahzaman slipped behind a tree, from where he could keep his eye on the party without being himself seen.

Presently he noticed the sultana detach herself from the group of women. She clapped her hands and called the name "Mesoud," softly but urgently, three times. It was then that Schahzaman saw a councillor by the name of Mesoud approach from a nearby pavilion. Taking the sultana by the hand he led her into the pavilion where the two embraced passionately.

"So," mused the prince, "I am not the only one to be betrayed. Even my brother has an untrustworthy wife."

Strangely enough, this unworthy thought cheered him up no end, so that by the time the sultan returned from the hunt that had taken him from the palace, he was looking much more carefree than he had since his arrival.

Schahriar immediately noticed the change in his brother and was encouraged to enquire the reason for the melancholy that had been so evident throughout his visit.

Reluctantly Schahzaman confessed that his sadness had been caused by the unfaithfulness of his wife and the terrible punishment he had meted out with his own hands.

"Well, now," exclaimed Schahriar, "were I thus wronged my fury would know no bounds. I would have sacrificed thousands in my anger; I swear it."

"But, tell me, brother; what has caused your sudden change of face? For weeks you have shown not a glimmer of a smile; have been silent and solitary. Now you have regained your spirits. Why now?"

Pressed further by the sultan, Prince Schahzaman reluctantly told the story of the sultana and her behaviour with Mesoud. It was then that a terrible madness came upon the sultan.

"Thousands will pay for this, I promise. But first my unfaithful wife and her lover!"

Sword in hand, he strode through the palace to the sultana's apartment and slew her without uttering a word. Mesoud was quickly summoned, and he too died by the sultan's sword.

"Never again," he vowed, "shall any wife deceive me. That is my oath, and all the world shall know it!"

Then Prince Schahzaman returned to Tartary, and his brother, the sultan Schahriar, began to fulfil his vow.

Scheherazade the Wise and Brave

The Sultan Schahriar, betrayed in love, set out to avenge himself on womankind. His plan was this. Each evening he commanded that one of the comeliest maidens in his kingdom be brought to the palace. There a wedding would take place with great ceremony and grandeur. A sumptuous feast would follow and the bride would be lavished with gifts. But the next morning at dawn the sultan would have her taken to the courtyard and beheaded.

It was the duty of the Grand Vizier to find a suitable bride each day; a task which the poor man found not only distasteful, but horrifying. Word of the sultan's cruel behaviour quickly spread across the land. Maidens who were blessed with beauty hid themselves in fear. Fathers spirited their daughters out of the city and sent them off to distant parts. The entire kingdom was in an uproar. The Grand Vizier was becoming demented. Not only did he hate his job, but daily it became more difficult to find a suitable victim. Pretty girls who were unable to flee the capital disfigured themselves or tried to disguise themselves as crones.

Now the Grand Vizier was himself the father of two daughters; the eldest was known as Scheherazade, and the younger was called Dinarzade. Although Dinarzade had no great beauty and few obvious talents to recommend her, Scheherazade was not only fair and beautiful to look upon, but was heroic, wise and resourceful. Moreover, she had been well schooled in all the branches of art, music and literature. She was a talented and much-sought-after person. It troubled her deeply to observe the terror to which young womanhood had been reduced in the city.

Daily, too, she witnessed her father's distress and increasing melancholy. One morning, unable to bear it any longer, she approached her father.

"I have a favour to ask of you, father," she said.

"Well, my daughter," he said, "what is your will? You know that I can refuse you nothing."

Taking her father by the arm and looking up into his face, Scheherazade said, "I am deeply troubled by what is happening to my sisters in this land. I am determined to put an end to the sultan's barbarous behaviour."

"There is nothing that would please me more," said her father. "But tell me, how do you propose to put a stop to it? You know that the sultan is our supreme ruler, and that his word is law."

"The answer is simple," said the girl resolutely. "It is your job to choose the sultan's brides. Well, let the next one be me."

"Have you taken leave of your senses, daughter?" cried the father. "How could I send you to your death? And how could marrying you to this fiend put an end to his madness?"

"Trust me, father. But I do have a plan. If I succeed, the country will be spared this cloud of fear and horror which hangs over it. Should I fail, I will at least have tried to save my sisters, and I shall die in the service of my countrywomen."

"No, child. I cannot allow it. You mean too much to me. It would be more than I could bear to lose you."

"Don't you think that every other father in the kingdom feels as you do? Why should we be spared? And, I assure you, father, I do have a plan which I'm sure will succeed." So the argument went on. The girl refused to heed her father's protests, and remained firm in her resolve to become the sultan's next bride.

At last the Grand Vizier had no argument left in him. He yielded to his daughter and mournfully announced to the sultan that the following afternoon he would be giving up his elder daughter, Scheherazade, to become the next wife of the sultan.

Even the sultan was astonished.

"You know what this means! Have you really made up your mind to sacrifice your daughter to me?"

"Your Highness, it is Scheherazade herself who insists. I seem to have no say in the matter."

The sultan was even more perplexed, but bade the Grand Vizier deliver his daughter to the bridal hall the next afternoon.

The distraught Vizier took back the news to Scheherazade, who appeared delighted, and in no way perturbed by the possibility of going to her doom. Rather, she bubbled with excitement and hastened to the courtyard where her sister, Dinarzade, was walking. Eagerly, she took the younger girl by the arm; "Sister," she said, "tomorrow I wed the sultan. No, don't look so dismayed. Everything will be fine. I have a plan; but I need you to help me."

"Good sister, how could I possibly help you?" asked Dinarzade. "Well you know what has befallen the unhappy brides of the sultan! How can you possibly agree to this monstrous marriage?"

"Fear not," Scheherazade assured the timid girl. "I'm sure that my plan will succeed. Then we shall have an end to all this horror, and maidens will be able to live without fear, and in peace again. Now listen; this is what I propose. After the wedding I will ask the sultan to allow you to attend me as I prepare for the night. I will tell him that you wish it, as do I." Then Scheherazade spoke in a whisper and confided the rest of her plan to Dinarzade.

The following morning Scheherazade was dressed in her wedding finery. Never had a bride looked lovelier. Even the sultan had a moment of regret as he looked on her beauty.

After the celebrations, and as the guests were leaving, Scheherazade spoke firmly to the sultan, "Your Highness, I would that my sister, Dinarzade, attend me this evening and sleep in our chamber this night. I would that one of my family and one who loves me be close by, on this my last night on earth."

"She has my permission," said the sultan.

So Dinarzade accompanied Scheherazade and her husband to the sultan's chamber, where they feasted royally and where the sultan drank freely.

An hour before dawn Dinarzade was ready to put her sister's plan into action. She went into the royal couple and spoke out in a firm, clear voice; "My dear sister, if this is to be our last hour together I beg you — tell me once again one of those special stories which you have shared with me so often before; one by which I shall always remember you."

Scheherazade made no answer. Dinarzade turned to the sultan. "Your Highness, will you permit my sister to share a story with me?"

"Yes. Yes. I have no objections," he answered, and to Scheherazade he said, "Let us hear your tale."

So Scheherazade began to speak. With quiet dignity she commenced her story. From the moment she began the sultan was entranced by the beauty of her voice and the manner of her telling. Soon he was caught in the spell of Scheherazade's story.

Dawn broke and the executioner and his guard could be heard gathering outside the royal chamber to take the new bride to her death.

Looking sideways at the sultan, Scheherazade broke off her telling and said, "There, that's all I have time for. The guard awaits, and I must go."

"No, wait," called the sultan. "Send the guard away. Finish your story."

"But not this morning, Your Highness, weariness overtakes me. Perhaps..."

"Yes indeed, why not let us have another day? Then tomorrow before dawn, you shall continue with the story. I must know what happens next."

Scheherazade's plan had worked. She had won a reprieve, and would go on doing so, for did she not have sufficient tales to extend for a thousand and one nights? Long before that, the maidens under the sultan's rule were rejoicing because they had been saved from their lord's cruel threat of execution.

As for Scheherazade and the sultan, by the time the storyteller had spun her thousand and one tales, the husband and wife had grown so accustomed to one another that the sultan couldn't bear to have his wife beheaded.

Boadicea: Queen of the Iceni

Although Boadicea, or Boudicca, is an historical figure mentioned in Book XIV of the Annals of the Roman historian Tacitus, written about 100 AD, little is known about her personally. Yet she is one of the most romantic heroines in the story of Britain. Tacitus heard her story from the lips of his father-in-law, Agricola, who was in Britain at the time of the Iceni rebellion. Cassius Dio, who was born about 155 AD and who draws heavily on Tacitus, also tells her story briefly.

A bronze statue of Boadicea riding in a scythed chariot was unveiled in 1902 on the banks of the River Thames at Westminster. In fact the chariots of the period consisted of two strong wheels, a long axle with a yoke for the harnessing of two horses, and an open wooden framework in which the driver stood, protected to a degree by wicker sides. There is no evidence of scythes being used on chariot wheels.

History does attest that in 60 AD Boadicea, who was the head of the Iceni, an East Anglian tribe, led a revolt against the Romans who had imposed sudden and crippling taxes, seized property and houses belonging to the British and carried off children as slaves or conscripts.

In those days Britain was in the hands of the ruthless Roman, the military leader, Seutonius Paulinus. His ambition was to subjugate the whole of the country to Rome. Wherever fugitives fled to escape his rule, Seutonius hunted them out. So when news came to him of refugees hiding on the island of Anglesey, which the Romans called Mona, Seutonius built flat-bottomed boats to carry his infantrymen across the shallows, while his cavalry followed, fording where possible, or swimming when the water became too deep.

On the island a dense array of armed British warriors waited along the shore. Women dressed in black, with dishevelled hair, screeching with rage and anguish, dashed among the ranks, stirring up the menfolk, while the Druids cursed aloud the oncoming Roman soldiers and lifted their hands to heaven in frenzied supplication.

Urged on by Seutonius and his generals, the Roman soldiers bore their standard implacably forward through the ranks of the resistance, wresting the flaming torches from the British and hurling them back until the crowd retreated with little fight left in them. The Britons had fiercely defended their homeland, but they proved no match for the might of the imperial Roman forces. The legionaries now ruthlessly followed up their victory by smashing up the sacred groves of the Druids and overthrowing their altars.

While Seutonius was occupied at Anglesey, word came to him of a sudden revolt in the province to the southeast, occupied by the Iceni, a rich independent farming people with great pride in their territory, which was still comparatively free of Roman oppression. Their ruler, Prasutagus, was a wealthy man and greatly concerned for the peaceful development of Icenia. He thought that by naming the Roman emperor, along with his two daughters, as one of his heirs his kingdom would not be over-run at his death, but that it would be allowed to develop in peace.

Unhappily, the reverse of what he expected happened. After his death in 59 AD a Roman force led by Catus and centurions from the colony at Colchester, or Camulodunum, joined with the Romans already in Icenia to seize the entire kingdom. The land and property of the Icenian noblemen were taken by force, and able-bodied young men, relatives of the king, were carried off as slaves. But worst of all, the widow of Prasutagus, whose name was Boadicea, was scourged and beaten, and her two daughters were assaulted and outraged. The Roman troops departed with as much loot as they could carry, and the soldiers of Catus went on a wild spree.

Boadicea's wrath was terrible to behold. She was a huge, well-built woman, with a sharp tongue and a loud voice, which, when raised in anger, brought fear to the hearts of her opponents. Her bright red hair fell in long tresses to her knees. A large gold chain and brooch held her outer mantle in place over her shoulders. She was to prove herself a robust and fiery warrior queen.

Conditions in Icenia now became intolerable for Boadicea. Her territory was reduced to the condition of a province of Rome. Crippling taxes were imposed, people were ejected from their homes and farms, and many were carried off as slaves. The occupying Roman soldiers showed no mercy to anyone who dared oppose them.

A Roman temple to the Divine Claudius was erected at Colchester, the capital of Roman Britain, and stood as a perpetual insult to the local people, and a symbol of tyranny.

The Britons began holding secret conferences, railing against the Roman yoke and stirring one another to action. Neighbouring tribes were kept informed by the Icenians who, under Boadicea, formed the rallying point for revolt.

Although the Romans had a well-developed intelligence service and a widespread network of spies, they knew nothing of the underground stirrings of the Icenians and their neighbours.

It was Boadicea herself who inspired the British by the force of her regal personality. She was able to bring a unity of purpose to tribes who previously had been at loggerheads. A secret army was being formed. Weapons were collected, stores were gathered and a campaign was planned.

The first objective of Boadicea was to capture Colchester, the centre of Roman culture. It was there that the hated temple stood and the centurions who had committed the outrage on Boadicea and the Icenians had their quarters.

While the army was being mustered there were reports of strange happenings at Colchester. "Without apparent reason," Tacitus wrote, "the Statue of Victory at Camulodunum fell down, with its back turned as though flying from the enemy. Women excited to frenzy prophesied impending destruction. Weird cries were heard in the Senate-house and inhuman wailings in the theatre. An image of the colony in ruins was seen in the estuary of the Tamesa. Even the ocean turned blood-red and the likenesses of human bodies left by the receding tide were interpreted as hopeful signs by the Britons, and omens of disaster by the veteran Romans."

The Romans became greatly alarmed. Their superstitions were stirred and they began worrying about the town's lack of defences. They planned the building of a moat and ramparts, but they never put their plans into action. The local Britons played a cunning game, appearing to be more passive and subservient than ever. The Romans were uneasy, but Seutonius was far away and Catus merely sent two hundred unarmed men to Colchester, where there was only a small military force. They assured themselves that all was well, in spite of the terrifying omens around them.

Meanwhile Boadicea was strengthening her forces with new recruits and inflaming the troops with fiery speeches, convincing them that they had the might to overthrow their enemy. Surrounding tribes such as the Trinovantes joined the Icenians, and one ancient report by Dio claims that Boadicea now commanded an army of 120,000 troops.

Although Seutonius had half the Roman army with him for his attack on Anglesey, there was a legion in Gloucester (Glevum), another on the upper Severn and another in Lincoln (Lindus). There were also occupied forts along the roads, and apart from the small detachment at Colchester there were also small forces at London (Londinium) and St. Albans (Verulamium).

But with Seutonius occupied with his campaign at Anglesey, the sacred island of the Druids, Boadicea knew that the time had come to attack. The Druid priests throughout the land, inflamed by Seutonius's attack on their island, supported her with subversive speeches, and urged the population to join her army.

It was in the spring that Boadicea mounted the rostrum in the midst of her host and made the call to battle. Wrote Dio, "She wore a great twisted golden necklace, and a tunic of many colours, over which was a thick mantle fastened by a brooch. Now she grasped a spear to strike fear into all who watched her." Her bright hair hung to her knees; her eyes blazed, her face was terrifying in its fury, and her voice became harsh with anger as she addressed the army and commanded it to attack.

The army poured down from the forests of Norfolk and Suffolk into Essex. The rebellion was no longer a secret. The military posts along the way were submerged by the mighty force of Britons. Messengers were sent galloping off by the Romans to inform Seutonius of what was happening. Boadicea in her chariot led her force straight to Colchester, which remained to her a symbol of her outrage and, to the British tribes, the hated centre of oppression. The women in her host were as determined as she was that victory and revenge would be theirs.

Tacitus tells us that the people of Colchester were surprised, as it were, in the midst of peace. They were surrounded by an immense host of what he called barbarians. The temple where the soldiers had gathered was stormed after a two-day siege. The town was sacked and plundered.

The victorious British army met Petilius Cerialis, commander of the ninth legion, as he was coming to the rescue, routed his troops, and destroyed all his infantry. Cerialis escaped with some of his cavalry, but, alarmed by this disaster and the fury of Boadicea and her army, the Roman Procurator, Catus, fled in disgrace across to Gaul.

After the capture and sacking of Colchester, Boadicea determined that she would occupy London. She well knew that the Romans would now rally all their forces, that they would never forgive the assault on their power and pride. Victory could not be assured until every Roman soldier had been killed or routed.

But by now word of the revolt had reached Seutonius at Anglesey. Seutonius made a quick decision. Colchester was lost; but London might be saved if he reached the town before Boadicea. Speed was essential. He rode off immediately with his cavalry, ordering the infantrymen to follow behind. Daring the hostile population, he made his way directly to London, which was then a strategic and prosperous trading centre. The river was full of shipping; wharves and warehouses lined its banks. Although it was a Roman centre, there were many Britons among its twenty thousand or more citizens. These Britons had accepted the Roman way of life and found it comfortable.

When Seutonius arrived with his weary cavalry he found the centre in anxious turmoil. Catus was in Gaul, so the citizens of London welcomed Seutonius as their saviour.

But Seutonius saw the situation differently. His infantrymen were still on their way. He knew that he could never hold the town against the oncoming British horde. If he withdrew he would have time to gather his army, the better to attack the British. He decided to save the whole province by sacrificing a single town. The tears and weeping of the people, as they implored his aid, left him unmoved in his decision. He took into his army all who would go with him.

The remainder of the population were left to fend for themselves against the oncoming force of Boadicea. Her army burst into London, hard on the heels of Seutonius, and there was an orgy of carnage and destruction. It is said that Roman women were skewered on long stakes. The Britons were not interested in taking prisoners, or making slaves of their victims. They were bent on slaughter, the gibbet, the fire and the cross. It was almost as if they knew their rampage would be brief. But for now, they would snatch instant revenge.

With London in ruins, the army of Boadicea immediately doubled back to St. Albans, where a similar sacking took place. On the way they attacked whatever fortresses and military garrisons lay in their path, and St. Albans was utterly destroyed.

Now the final battle had to be fought, in which Boadicea and her force would meet Seutonius and his army. But while the British were marching on St. Albans, Seutonius had gathered up the fourteenth legion and a detachment of veterans from the twentieth, with other auxiliary troops numbering some ten thousand men.

The Roman leader decided to make an end to delay, and fight. He carefully chose a position approached by a narrow pass, closed in behind by a forest. Before him was an open plain, so there could be no danger of ambush. The British forces were approaching directly. He was safe at the rear.

The legions of Seutonius were in close array. They were flanked by light-armed troops. The cavalry waited tensely in the wings.

The British army, with its masses of infantry and cavalry, were in a confident mood. Their numbers had been increased and they had brought with them their wives, riding in wagons, to witness the victory they were sure would be theirs.

Boadicea, with her two daughters beside her in the chariot visited each of the tribes.

"It may not be usual for Britons to fight under the leadership of women," she told them. "But now, it is not as a woman of noble ancestry that I lead you, but as one of the people. I am avenging lost freedom, my scourged body, the outraged chastity of my daughters. Roman lust has gone so far that not even old age or youth has been spared its assaults. But heaven is on the side of a righteous

102

vengeance. A legion that has dared to fight has perished. The remainder are hiding themselves in their camp, or are thinking anxiously of flight. They will not resist even the noise and shouting of so many thousands, let alone our attack and our force. If you consider well the strength of our army, the causes of the war, you will see that in this battle you must conquer or die. This is a woman's resolve. As for men, they may live and be slaves if they wish.''

The men cheered wildly when they heard this exhortation. For those who could not hear, there was the vision of Boadicea driving through their ranks in her chariot with her long hair streaming and her daughters by her side — testimony to the truth of what she was saying.

At the Roman camp Seutonius was also rallying his troops. He laughed to scorn the presumption of the barbarians. "There," he said, "you see more women than warriors. Unwarlike, unarmed, they will give way the moment they experience the weapons and courage of troops which have so often routed them before. In any army of many legions, it is the few who decide the outcome. What glory will come to you, a small band that fights for the honour of the entire army! Close up your ranks. Discharge your javelins. Then with shields and swords continue the work of bloodshed and destruction. Do not pause for plunder. With victory, everything will come to you!''

Such enthusiasm followed the general's address, and so promptly did the veteran army prepare for the hurling of their javelins, that it was with utter confidence in the result that Seutonius gave the signal for battle.

The legionaries discharged their javelins with unerring aim on the closely approaching Britons. They were in line, five or six ranks deep. As the soldiers in the front line hurled their weapons they immediately reached to their companions behind them in the second rank and seized a new javelin to follow the first. And so the manoeuvre proceeded.

The Britons were charging up a slope and their front men were quickly struck down by the Roman missiles. Soon, bodies were piling on bodies. The Roman auxiliaries then closed in, while the cavalry, with extended lances, crushed all further resistance. Boadicea's army was in disarray. Flight was difficult, because the surrounding wagons blocked any possible retreat. The Romans spared no one; not least of all the women. The British horses and beasts of burden swelled the piles of bodies. Seutonius was exultant.

It was reported that little fewer than eighty thousand Britons fell that day, with a loss of about four hundred Roman soldiers, and only as many wounded. The revolt was over. Two thousand legionaries, eight cohorts of auxiliaries and a thousand cavalry were sent across from Germany to help put an end to the rebellion. Famine did the rest. In the frenzy of their opposition to the Romans, the British tribesmen had been careless in planting their crops for the summer. Boadicea's courageous stand and its aftermath resulted in the greatest loss that

Britain has ever suffered.

As for Boadicea and her daughters, they were last seen by the Romans driving in their chariot with the British army. Tacitus records bluntly, "Boadicea put an end to her life by poison." Dio says that she returned to her own territory and died of disease.

Perhaps it is of little importance. She will always be remembered as a commanding, indomitable spirit who fought valiantly for the freedom of herself and her people.

Joan of Arc

Joan of Arc was born at Domrémy in Champagne, the daughter of a peasant farmer, probably in 1412. She was burnt at the stake for heresy, witchcraft and sorcery in 1431. George Bernard Shaw, who wrote a play about her, calls her "the most notable Warrior Saint in the Christian calendar".

Joan grew up during the Hundred Years' War, during which English armies overran most of France. Henry V of England had taken advantage of civil strife in France to revive Edward III's claim to the throne of that country. Henry landed in Normandy in 1415 with a force of about thirty thousand soldiers, and engaged an army of French nobility at Agincourt in which battle ten thousand Frenchmen perished — it was one of the bloodiest battles of the Middle Ages.

In 1422 both Henry V and Charles VI of France, who was mad, died within three months of one another. The child, Henry VI, was then claimed "by the grace of God" to be "King of France and of England". France was in ruins. An English regent, the Duke of Bedford, governed in Paris. The country was divided. On the one hand, there was a ten-month-old child who was not French, but who had been proclaimed king of France. On the other hand, there was the new king, Charles VII, who was still known as the Dauphin, as he had not been crowned and consecrated. He was a weak and timid youth, controlled by dishonest and selfish counsellors, and incapable of leading his people.

Although the Duke of Bedford had tried to win the French over by behaving "correctly" and through capable administration, he was still opposed by the city of Orleans, to which he laid siege. Charles, the ruler of Orleans, was a prisoner of the English, and the city defended itself heroically. The people of Orleans were praying that God's judgement would be in their favour and that they would be delivered from the English. It was then that Joan of Arc appeared.

As the notes of the Angelus bell travelled across the clear evening air, a young maiden who was making her way through the fields to the farmhouse, where she lived with her father and mother and brothers, fell reverently to her knees. Making the sign of the cross, she began to recite the Rosary. But even as the familiar words fell from her lips her mind darkened, and her thoughts wandered to what she had heard spoken of in the village, on her way home from Mass, the previous Sunday.

"Our Father in Heaven, may I always be an instrument of your will." And her mind cried out, "Holy Mary, blessed Michael the archangel, Saint Catherine and dear Saint Margaret, pray for me and my beloved France, I beg of you. Come to our aid in this time of great trouble. God give strength to the Dauphin that he may resist the English, these foreigners, who have invaded our country."

Darkness was falling as she picked her way across the furrows. Her mind was still busy, turning over what she had recently heard spoken of in her village of Domrémy. The menfolk and the women could be heard murmuring against Queen Isabeau. "Flighty," they said of her, "and extravagant. A foreigner from Bavaria." They blamed her for the king's madness. Poor Charles VI, who had died two years ago! And that boy, the Dauphin, had not yet been anointed with the holy oil, and France was in ruins.

Joan, for that was the maid's name, sighed deeply. What could she, a poor peasant girl from Lorraine, do to help France? They said, in the village, that because it was a woman who had brought about this pass, God would send another woman to right the wrongs that had been done, not only by the English, but by their weak and dishonest countrymen. That was hard to take, the folly of good Frenchmen. What sort of woman could speak out against the weakness of men? A maiden, they said. "What if I were to be the chosen one?" Joan quickly pushed that thought from her mind, and went in to greet her mother and father. For all her troubled thoughts, she ate a hearty supper, and slept soundly in her comfortable bed the whole night through.

Early the next morning Joan woke as the sun beamed in through her window. It was summer, and gloriously fresh and warm. Gone were her gloomy thoughts of the evening before. She even sang as she dressed, and chattered away as she ate her simple breakfast of fresh bread, with milk from her father's cow.

All that morning she worked in the garden, weeding, hoeing and raking. She was strong, and just fourteen — what was hard work to her? Why, she could work all day in the sun if need be, and not feel tired.

Then at midday the Angelus again rang out and Joan knelt in the garden to pray. It was then that she heard her name called three times, and each call was in a different voice. They were not voices that she had ever heard before. She looked around, but there was not a person in sight. That did not surprise the girl, for the voices came from within her head. Again she heard her name. Two female voices and that of a man.

A great fear came upon the maid. Who was calling her? Was she ill? Was she perhaps going mad? Then they called again; "Joan! Joan! Joan! You are the maid. You *are* the maid!" Then they were silent. A small bird chirped at her from the bough of one of the fruit trees, and looked at the girl knowingly. They were such sweet voices, good and kind. There was nothing to be afraid of. Perhaps they would come again. She must listen to what they said; for surely they were sent from God. Yes, God himself would talk to her through her Voices.

And he did, not once, but many times. The seasons came and went, and although life in the countryside around Domrémy went on as it always did, things in the outside world only grew worse. Only a few small towns in the east of France held out for the Dauphin, who had still not been crowned king. Four harvests had been gathered in since Joan first heard her Voices.

In the village, talk still went on. "There will come a maid," they insisted. "There is an old prophecy that France will be saved in time of trouble by a maiden from the Oakwood. And isn't there the great oak wood just outside the village? Could it be a maiden from Domrémy who will now save France?"

Deep in her heart Joan knew who that maiden was. Her beloved Voices were coming to her more frequently. She heard them in the garden, and particularly in the fields, when she prayed at the hour of the Angelus. Once, when she was guarding her flock at midday, the sun seemed suddenly to glow more brightly. A great light had flooded down upon her as she prayed and there, above her, appeared the Archangel Michael, Saint Catherine and Saint Margaret, smiling, but speaking firmly to her. "Go," they said, "to the Dauphin. He needs you, for he must deliver Orleans from the enemy. God himself is ordering this thing, and it is fitting that you should do His will. You are the maid."

At last Joan knew that the time had come for her to obey her divine command. She could delay no longer. She had spoken long and earnestly with her parents. The priest had given her his blessing. Now she had to go to the castle of Vaucoleurs, where Captain Robert de Beaudricourt was in command of a French garrison that was still loyal to the Dauphin.

It was a fine morning in the spring of 1429 when Joan, in her simple red dress, was at last shown into the captain's presence. Well she knew that she was doing what her Voices bade her, and she was in no way afraid of the captain. She approached him confidently, then curtseyed. "Good morning, captain squire. I have come to you with orders from my lord. You are to give me a horse and armour, and a band of soldiers to go with me to the Dauphin."

"So you say, my girl. But who is your lord, that he makes such demands on Captain de Beaudricourt? Who are you, anyway?"

"My lord is the king of heaven; and I am his maid, Joan. I have a message from God for the Dauphin, and you must help me deliver it."

"Must I? Not so fast, my girl. What is this message for the Dauphin? How do I know that it is God who sends you to me?"

"I am sent by God because Blessed Michael, the Archangel, and the dear saints Catherine and Margaret have spoken to me, often. It is the will of God that the Dauphin risk no battle just yet. Before the middle of Lent next year God will send help. But the Dauphin must be crowned, and I am to lead him from Chinon to Reims where he will be anointed with the holy oil. He must then give me soldiers to raise the siege of Orleans."

"You, head an army? What do you know of warfare, a lass from Lorraine?"

"At Domrémy, which is my village, we had to flee to escape the English soldiers. I have seen them with my own eyes. And I have heard tales of their Black Prince, who is possessed by the devil. It is the will of God that he be driven away, back to his own country, and that France be free of the English forever."

For all her pleading, Joan could not persuade the captain that what she said was true. It was with sadness in her heart that she returned home as she was bade to do, but deep down she knew that she would return.

And so she did. In the middle of Lent in 1429 Joan turned her back on Domrémy, which she was never to see again, and went once more to de Beaudricourt.

"You delay too long," she told him. "On this very day, at Orleans, the Dauphin has lost a battle. This is a sign from heaven, and I must go to him."

It was indeed true that the Dauphin had lost a battle — the Battle of Herrings, so called because the English defeated and cut off a French force that attacked them as they were bringing herrings into the camp with provisions for Lent. Yet Joan was many miles away, and she could have heard nothing directly of this battle.

So de Beaudricourt was convinced. The people now brought clothes for Joan to wear on her journey to Chinon and the Dauphin. They were such clothes as were worn by men — doublet, hose, surcoat, boots, spurs — and Robert de Beaudricourt gave the maid a sword.

Into the chill morning air of the twenty-third day of February 1429 rode seven travellers from the gate of the castle at Vaucoleurs. There were two squires and their attendants, and Joan, the maiden from Domrémy. To the young squires, Joan appeared to be an angel, and the company travelled towards Chinon in a state of awe and wonder. It was a dangerous journey, for English soldiers roamed the countryside. They would stand no opposition from the French, peasants or gentry.

On 6 March Joan arrived at Chinon. She requested that she be taken at once to the Dauphin. For three days the Dauphin's advisers refused to allow her into his presence. But God was on her side, and at last she was ushered into the vast hall where Charles was surrounded by his great lords and the nobility.

"Let us test the maid," said the Dauphin to his courtiers. "Let me stand among you, as one of you, and let us see if the maid has divine vision."

All eyes were on Joan as she walked in her male attire through that huge assembly. She walked straight up to Charles and saluted him.

"Why do you salute me, child? I am not the king. Yonder he stands," said Charles pointing to one of his courtiers, "salute him."

"Nay, gentle Dauphin, you cannot fool me. You are he!"

Still Charles hesitated. Joan was so sure, but he was so uncertain. Not so, many of the court. In Chinon, Joan stayed in the house of a noble lady, and the young Duc de Alençon accompanied her everywhere. He was astonished by her horsemanship, and full of admiration for the courage of the girl. The great of the city came to visit her and she told them humbly that she was sent by God. When she was alone she wept and prayed, but in the presence of the Dauphin she stood firm and resolute.

At last she said to him, "Do you need a miracle to believe in me and so to believe in yourself? Let me tell you something known only to you and to God." The maid bent low and spoke in a soft voice, then added, "You are the true son of the late king and the rightful heir to the throne of France. I tell you, before God, I am sent to drive away the English from Orleans and from France, and to crown you king in the cathedral at Reims, where are crowned all true kings of France."

Something of Joan's fire entered the soul of the poor, weak, uncrowned king, and he began to believe in Joan. In that way he *could* believe in himself; for a while, anyway. His mind was made up. "I will give you command of the army. Do what you will with it!" he told her.

Jean and Pierre, Joan's brothers, were summoned from Domrémy to ride with her at the head of an army to Orleans. It was a shame-faced Charles who gave Joan armour to wear in battle, and he offered her a sword.

As so often at important times in her life, Joan's Voices sounded insistently and clearly. They told her about a church, where behind the altar was an ancient sword, with five crosses on the blade, buried in the earth. That was the sword she was to wear.

A man whom Joan had never seen before was sent from Tours and commissioned to seek the sword. He found it exactly in the place that the maid had described, and the people shouted for joy.

Joan commanded that a standard be embroidered for her, bearing the words JESUS MARIA and the fleur-de-lis, the lilies of France, on a white field. This banner, she insisted, meant more to her than her sword. She did not hate the English; she only wanted them out of France so that Frenchmen could live undisturbed lives once more among their fields and vineyards.

Still the Dauphin was hesitant and fearful.

"Why do you doubt?" Joan asked him. "Do not listen to your counsellors.

Follow me, and let me lead you to Reims, to assume your worthy crown."

Even then Charles paid heed to those who hated the maid, and Joan saw time slipping by.

"I shall be with you for but a year," she told the king and his counsellors. The people began to murmur. "She will be with us for but a year. Why do we hesitate?"

When at last Joan went to war, it is said that she led over ten thousand soldiers. She was then seventeen.

The people of Orleans had long been holding out against the besieging English. Their provisions were running out and their spirits were low. Joan used her army to defend a great convoy of provisions for the beleaguered city. When she arrived at the city with her army and succeeded in entering it, the people crowded around her, blessing her and trying to kiss the hand of the maiden from Domrémy.

At dawn the next morning Joan attacked the castle. The French and Scottish soldiers leaped into the foss, set their ladders against the walls, and scaled to the battlements where the English waited with their swords and axes. Cannonballs, great stones and arrows rained down upon them. "Fight on," called the maid, "the place is ours!"

Early in the afternoon Joan set a ladder against the wall with her own hands, and began to mount it. An arrow pierced clean through her armour between neck and shoulder, wounding her. Joan cried out, but seized the arrow and with her hands dragged it out. Yet she did not withdraw from the battle, or seek medical help.

The onslaught lasted all day, and the French cause seemed hopeless. When night fell the maid mounted her horse, rode into a vineyard where she prayed for seven or eight minutes. Then she returned, seized her banner, and strode to the brink of the foss.

The English were smitten with fear when they saw her. When the French charged again, they met with little resistance. The English fled, or were slain; and the French returned gladly to the city of Orleans. The next day the English were routed.

Joan rode victorious to Chinon and urged the king to allow her to take him to Reims and crown him. When he delayed, she begged him not to hold so many councils. "Come to Reims, and receive your crown," she implored him.

When the king still would not move, Joan fell to prayer, and her Voices reassured her. "Daughter of God, go on. He will help you," they told her.

Joan was joyful, and gave thanks, but she repeated to the Dauphin, "Make haste, for I am with you for but one year, or a little more. Use me while you may."

That one year was sadly wasted. Charles loitered about the castle with his favourites and weak-willed advisers. Joan fought other battles, and won. Wherever she went, the French were victorious.

At long last, and with great difficulty, in July of 1429 Charles was led to Reims, there to be crowned in the tradition of his ancestors. As the holy oil was poured Joan stood beside the king, with her standard in her hand. "It bore the brunt," she said, "and deserves to share the renown."

When the ceremony was over and the king was crowned and anointed, Joan knelt weeping at his feet.

"Gentle King," she said, "now is fulfilled the will of God, who desired that you should come to Reims to receive your worthy anointing and consecration, and to prove that you are the true king and that the kingdom is yours."

But in that day of triumph, Joan was deeply sad. "I would to God that I could now lay down my arms and return to my mother and father and serve them by watching their sheep, but that is not to be. There is still work for me to do, although the time be short."

The king bade Joan choose her reward. Already she had been given horses, finely wrought armour, and jewelled daggers. Much of what was given to her she gave to the poor. She wanted money only to wage her ruler's wars, not for herself.

Her family was made noble. On its shield, between two lilies, a sword upholds a crown. Her father was in Reims and saw her in her glory. He was able to take home with him the joyful news that as her reward from the king for all her valiant endeavours, Joan had chosen that her home village of Domrémy be free of taxes.

Now her great desire was to return the king to his capital. Sadly, her attack on Paris was a failure. In the assault of September 1429 she was wounded in the thigh. Throughout the winter that followed Joan champed with impatience. The king, now crowned Charles VII, was still slow to be moved. There were many who were jealous of Joan, and some who hated her.

Nevertheless, the maid pressed on. She was determined to go to the relief of Compiègne, which was besieged by the Burgundians, who were allies of the English. Undaunted by the great odds against her, Joan led a sortie from the gates, but was cut off from the main body of troops when the gates were closed behind her, probably through treason. Without any to help her, Joan was captured and imprisoned by the Duke of Burgundy. Charles made no attempt to save her, and the Burgundians, who had no great love for France, sold the maid who had rescued Orleans to the English.

To the English, Joan was a witch — a girl who wore male armour, who carried a standard and rode into battle urging on the soldiers, like any other commander, could be nothing else. Besides, many were the stories and the rumours about the Voices; and they spread far and wide, among both the French and the English.

And how could a farmer's daughter whisper secrets to the king of France and stand beside him while he was being crowned and consecrated? Surely she must be in league with unseen forces and had cast a spell on Charles. If her powers were not from God — and to the English who had suffered defeat because of the maid, how could they be? — then they must be of the devil. So Joan must be a witch, and a heretic. And in those days the punishment for such a crime was death by fire — to be burnt at the stake.

So Joan, who had obeyed her Voices and who for love of France had led an army to victory, was fettered and imprisoned at Rouen. There she was brought before an ecclesiastical court to be tried for witchcraft and heresy by the Bishop of Beauvais, Pierre Cauchon. The bishop carefully chose judges, seventy-five in all, whom he knew would bring a verdict against Joan.

For months Joan was subjected to harsh questioning by men whose minds were already made up that she must die. Yet Joan's Voices were still with her. "Answer boldly," they told her. In the quiet of her cell the lass from Domrémy continued to pray, day by day, hour by hour. Even when she could no longer hear the Angelus ringing she lifted her heart to God. "In three months," her Voices told her, "you will be free, with great victory, and you will enter the kingdom of Paradise."

So Joan did answer boldly, and at times some of the inquisitors were strangely and deeply troubled. But they could not swim against the tide that was sweeping Joan to destruction.

In the spring of 1431 Joan was led out into the cemetery of St. Ouen where a huge crowd had gathered, shouting and clamouring for her death. Dressed now in the simple dress of a peasant girl, she stood defenceless before the multitude.

The wily bishop, Cauchon, had prepared a paper for Joan to sign. "Recant," he told her. "Only say that your Voices were of the devil, and we will forgive you."

Beyond the cemetery, in the market place, a stake had been hammered into the ground. Great mounds of twigs and branches were piled high around it. The crowd of priests, prelates and people were calling for Joan's death.

A pen was thrust into Joan's hand. "Make your mark, quickly," the bishop told her. "Renounce your blasphemy and promise never to wear man's clothing again, and never more give way to the temptations of demons."

It is said that Joan made her mark, her hand guided by that of the inquisitor. Who knows what mark was made or by whom?

Some say, too, that the inquisitor hissed into Joan's ear, "To earn the forgiveness of the Church and Almighty God we condemn you to imprisonment for the remainder of your earthly days."

It was then that Joan's voice was heard rising above the babble of the crowd: "My Voices were right. They told me not to trust you. How could I live my days in darkness away from the blue of the sky and the sun in the heavens? Burn me. Do away with me. God is my refuge. In him I trust. Better the kingdom of Paradise than hell on earth.''

Already the fire in the market place had been kindled. Its glow was turning the May sunshine red. Joan was hustled away. She had time only to put on her male attire, her wartime garments, before being led to the market place, and tied to the stake.

The burning branches were pushed closer to ignite the pyre around her. Joan looked once at the crowd, her eyes sweeping their faces with a look of calm forgiveness.

A soldier who was standing by felt his heart move within him. Reaching down he took two sticks and quickly bound them to form a cross. Leaping forward he thrust the symbol of deliverance into the maid's hands.

Through the flames Joan could be seen holding the cross as high as her bound arms would allow her, her face turned upward, looking towards the heavens. Amid the roar of the fire came the sound of one name: Jesus. And the maid from Domrémy was no more. Her ashes were to be thrown into the Seine.

Joan was burnt on 30 May 1431, when she was nineteen. Charles VII had done nothing to save her. Some twenty years later her family asked for her case to be re-opened. In 1456 a commission of enquiry quashed the original verdict and declared Joan's innocence. In 1920 Pope Benedict XV canonised her — declared her to be a saint. Churches throughout the world have been dedicated in her honour, and a statue of her stands in Winchester Cathedral in England. Many books have been written about her, including a play by George Bernard Shaw, *St. Joan*, first published in 1924. Even those who still doubt Joan's Voices agree that she is proof of the miracles that can be achieved through an unyielding will and fervent faith.

The Hunter Maiden of the Zuñi People

L ong ago in North America in the days of the ancients, there lived at the Little Gateway of the Zuñi River a young Indian maiden. She lived alone with her aged and feeble parents in their pueblo. Her brothers had been slain in wars, so it fell to the maiden to supply the household with food and fuel.

The girl was an able gardener and in the summer she grew beans, pumpkins, squash, melons and corn to feed the small family. In those days her people kept neither sheep nor cattle, and their only meat came from what they hunted for themselves. Sometimes the girl would barter vegetables for meat; but as she could grow scarcely enough for her family's own needs, there was little enough to exchange. So when winter came she and her parents were left to exist on only dried beans and corn.

In the years when her brothers were alive they used to take their stone axes and rabbit sticks to hunt for meat. Now their weapons hung unused on the walls of the pueblo, for the father was too aged and infirm to hunt, and it was frowned on for womenfolk to do so.

One snowy late-autumn day the maiden was gathering brush and firewood and piling it along the roof of the pueblo. Looking down from the roof, she saw the young men of the village going out to the hunt·with their stone axes and rabbit sticks. Later in the day she watched as they returned with long strings of rabbits — not one of them was empty-handed.

It was then that she decided, woman or not, that the very next day she herself would go hunting. "Then my mother and my father will have fresh meat to cheer them up and put flesh on their lean bodies," thought the girl to herself. "When I

115

was a child, did I not go with my brothers on their hunting expeditions? It should not be hard to track the rabbits through the snow, I'm sure that I can do it."

Her mind made up, the maiden spoke that night to her aged parents, as they sat by the fireplace warming themselves. "My dear parents, today the snow has fallen and the young men have already gone hunting rabbits. We have nothing with which to barter for meat. So tomorrow I will go myself and track the rabbits through the snow and hunt them down with my brother's weapons."

"*Naiya*, daughter," said the old woman, shaking her head. "It is too cold. You would become lost in the mountains, or grow too weary. Hunting is not woman's work."

"It is true," added her father. "Only men go hunting. It would be better for us to stay hungry and live in poverty than for you to run such risks as you are suggesting, O my daughter."

Say what her parents would, the girl had made up her mind. "The stone axes and rabbit sticks of my brothers hang on the wall. There is no reason why I shouldn't use them," she insisted.

At last the old man gave way and said, "Very well! You will do as you say. But I will help you as best I can."

He hobbled into the next room and returned with a pile of old deerskins covered with thick fur. These he moistened and softened; then he cut out long stockings from them, which he stitched with the sinew and fibre of the yucca leaf. Then he selected for the maiden a number of her brothers' rabbit sticks and a heavy stone axe.

While he was doing this, the old woman busied herself preparing a lunch for the girl, of corn cakes spiced with pepper and wild onions. When the cakes had been baked in the ashes she strung them on yucca fibre, like beads on thread, and laid them down beside the axe and the rabbit sticks and the deerskin stockings.

Early the next morning, well before the young men were awake, the girl dressed herself warmly, drew on her deerskin stockings, then threw the string of corn cakes over her shoulder and stuck the rabbit sticks into her belt. Carrying the stone axe in her hand she set out through the Gateway of Zuñi for the Plain of the Burned River, so called because of the black, charred-looking rocks along its banks. The snow stretched dazzling white before her, fresh and unbroken until she reached the northern end of the valley, where she picked up the trail of many rabbits, dodging in and out of bushes and among the rocks.

Eagerly she ran from one place to another. Because she was inexperienced as a hunter, at first she caught nothing. Then she had the good fortune to run some rabbits into a hollow log. As she had seen her brothers do years before, she quickly split the log, dug out the rabbits and killed them with a swift blow of her hand on the nape of the neck, behind the ears.

For each rabbit she breathed a sigh of thankfulness. Now her parents would be well fed and would grow strong again. "I can dry some of the meat, and it will last many days," she thought to herself.

When the snow began to fall, she failed to notice it, so intent she was on her hunting. It began to grow dark. Still she took no note of it; and the string of rabbits grew heavier and heavier across her shoulders.

Only when the snow fell steadily and it was too dark to see did she realise that she could no longer follow her own trail. She was lost and alone in a snowy landscape. And indeed, the maiden was moving southward across the valley instead of going eastward along it.

"Well," she thought to herself, "I shall have to find shelter among the rocks. If I stay here for the night it will stop snowing, and I will be able to go home in the morning."

Even as she was thinking this she saw a black mass standing out against the whiteness of the snow. Groping her way forward she found that she had come to the base of a cliff. Stretching out her free hand she felt her way along the cliff face until she came to an opening. Unwittingly, she had stumbled upon what is known as Taiuma's Cave.

"Here I will shelter," she thought. As she crawled into the cave she saw a glowing light, which indeed turned out to be the embers of a fire. Beside the fire were piles of broken wood and pine cones sufficient to keep a fire blazing throughout the night.

"So," she thought. "Other rabbit-hunters have been here before me. I'll soon make use of what they have left."

It was not long before the fire was crackling, then burning steadily. Its heat began to warm her and she danced about in glee. Spreading her mantle on the floor of the cave she began to dry herself off. Then she took a rabbit, dressed it and began to roast it by a spit on the fire. While it was cooking she untied the string of her mother's corn cakes and prepared for her solitary feast. Soon she was eating heartily, thinking how fortunate she was to have discovered not only shelter, but the warmth of fire. After she had had her fill she settled down for a good night's sleep, confident that she would be able to find her way home in the morning.

Then it was that the quiet and stillness of the cave was broken by a distant, long, low cry of distress — "Ho-o-o-o thlaia-a!" — coming from outside.

"Ah," thought the maiden, "it is another hunter lost in the snow." Rising up, she made her way to the mouth of the cave, and called out in answer.

Again, but nearer and louder, came the call. The girl ran out from the cave calling loudly, "Li-i thlaia-a! Here, here!"

Once again came the call, but closer at hand; and it was followed by a loud clattering and rattling. A huge shadow lunged towards her.

In terror and dismay she turned and ran back to the entrance of the cave. This

118

could be none other than the Cannibal Demon, who had seen the light of her fire and had come to devour her. The shadowy shape came even closer, and the rattling sound grew more intense. The girl retreated further into the cave. Still the shadow approached, until it seemed to block the entire entrance to the cave. A loud, harsh voice called from the darkness, "Ho lithlsh tâ ime! So there you are, inside, are you!"

The terrified girl moved back even further. From the entrance to the cave she could hear the menacing voice calling, "Let me in. I'm cold and hungry. Let me in, I tell you!"

Not a word did the girl answer. The shape moved as though to come into the cave, but it was too bulky to fit through the entrance. The giant shoulders would not squeeze in.

Then the voice changed. It became slyly civil. "Come out here, and bring me something to eat."

"I've not anything to give you," called the girl. "I've eaten all my food. There is nothing left."

"What about the rabbits I can smell?" came the voice.

So the girl threw out a rabbit, which the monster caught in his long, claw-like hand. In one swallow it had disappeared down the creature's throat.

"Throw me another!" he demanded.

And the girl did.

"And another! And another!" One by one the girl tossed away her precious rabbits, until not one remained. Each one the monster caught and swallowed, hair and all, in one great gulp.

"Throw me some more."

"I have no more. That was the last. Go away!"

"Then throw me your deerskin stockings!" These, too, the Demon devoured. "Your moccasins".

"Your belt. Your mantle. Your blanket."

Soon there was nothing left for the girl to throw. Now the bloated demon had no hope of ever squeezing or levering his way through the opening.

So, raising a great flint axe he proceeded to batter at the stone of the entrance. Chips of stone began to flake away. The chunks of rock broke off. Pound, pound, pound, hammer, hammer, hammer. The blows rang through the darkness outside, and filled the cave, like the sound of pounding water in a storm.

Far away, on Thunder Mountain, the sound of the pounding hammer travelled to where two war gods were sitting quietly talking. They knew at once that it was the axe of the Cannibal Demon, and that he was causing trouble.

Catching up their weapons, they flew at once through the darkness to the cliff face, where the monster was still hammering at the entrance to the cave.

Now, war gods watch over the affairs of humans. They knew that the maiden

119

had gone hunting for the sake of her aged parents and that she had braved the perils of the night on their behalf. As soon as they arrived at the cave they knew what was happening.

The maiden had almost fainted away at the sight of the great, ugly face, the grizzly hair, the staring, bloodshot eyes, the yellow tusks and the talon-like hands of the Demon. But with two swift blows from the war gods' clubs the apparition was felled to the ground, dead.

"You have no more to fear, good maiden," they called. "Rest now, by the fire. We shall sleep at the entrance to the cave and watch over you until the morning."

So the maiden slept; and in the morning the war gods woke her gently. Then they told her many things; and taught her much that she had not before known. They praised her for her courage and her skill. Finally they said to her, "Return now to your Village of the Gateway of the River of Zuñi: on the way we will slay rabbits beyond number for you. We will go with you all the way down the snowy valley, and when you are within sight of your parent's pueblo we will leave you."

As they walked through the fresh, untrodden snow, the gods continued to instruct the girl in the ways of hunting. Much wisdom did they impart to her. When they could see the smoke rising from the houses of the girl's village the war gods turned to her and handed her the heavy strings of rabbits which they carried. Then the gods were seen no more.

Glowing from within, the maiden walked proudly through the village, bearing the strings of rabbits on her shoulders. The village folk gazed on her in awe and wonder. Every hunter in the village knew that he could not compare with such a huntress. Never had they seen such a catch!

The girl glanced neither to right nor to left. She strode through the village folk to the pueblo where her old parents sat mourning her loss. All night they had kept watch, but with morning their hope had slowly ebbed away, like the departing tide.

While she prepared a rabbit for the pot to feed her parents the girl told them all that had happened to her. "Many dangers have I endured this past night. I know now what it is to hunt like a man. But I have learnt much from the gods. When the time comes, I will marry and my man will hunt rabbits and deer for you, and for me and my children."

The hunter maiden, as she became known among the Zuñi people, soon had no need to hunt alone. One youth, bolder than his brothers, who had long admired the beauty of the maiden, presented himself, with a bundle, at the maiden's fireside. And she was wise enough to accept him.

Vasilissa the Beautiful

Far off in the heart of Russia, there once lived a merchant who married for the second time a widow of about his own age who had two daughters of her own.

By his first wife the merchant had had but one child, a daughter, who from her cradle was known as Vasilissa the Beautiful.

Before she died, Vasilissa's mother had called her daughter to her bedside and, taking a tiny wooden doll from under the blankets, had put it into Vasilissa's hands saying;

"My own dear daughter, listen carefully and never forget what I am about to say. This doll is my dying gift to you. It is most precious, because there is no other like it in the world. Keep it always hidden in your pocket, and never show it to anyone. Should evil or misfortune come your way, take out the doll and secretly give it something to eat and drink. It will take a little food and drink; after which you will be able to tell it your troubles. Then it will advise you how to act." The good woman kissed her daughter, and shortly afterwards died.

So grievously did the child mourn for her mother that in the dark of the night she took hold of her little doll, and set before it a small piece of bread and a sip of beer.

"There my little doll; eat a little and drink a little, for great is my misfortune now that my mother is dead."

At these words the doll's eyes lit up like fireflies and it stirred into life. After it had eaten a crumb of the bread and swallowed a sip of beer it said; "Stop crying, little Vasilissa. Grief is always worse at night. Lie down and go to sleep and things will be better in the morning, I promise you."

And so they were, until Vasilissa's father remarried. The girl's new mother was a cruel woman, and her two daughters, who were as sombre and ugly as two crows, were jealous of Vasilissa's beauty.

Between them, the three women made Vasilissa's life a misery. She became nothing but a household drudge, running errands in the snow and rain, dusting and sweeping the house and tending to the kitchen fire.

When life became too burdensome Vasilissa would creep into a closet in the dark of night and set before her little doll a morsel of food and something to drink.

Always the little doll's eyes would light up like fireflies, and it would come alive. It would unfailingly comfort the distraught girl and tell her how to act.

Often when Vasilissa stepped into the kitchen in the morning she would find that the little doll had already set and kindled the fire, drawn a fresh pail of water, and put the kitchen to rights. In many ways she helped lighten the poor girl's burden, and whatever joy came into Vasilissa's life was there because of her mother's dying gift.

As the years passed, Vasilissa grew even more beautiful, while her step-sisters remained faded and so unattractive in looks and disposition that the young men of the village gave them a wide berth. But to Vasilissa they were attracted like flies to a honey-pot.

But when any one of them proposed marriage the step-mother flew into a storm of anger, driving the suitor away, and declaring, "Never shall Vasilissa wed before my daughters. Are they not older than she is?" And she would flog the girl in anger and spite. So, but for her little doll, Vasilissa was alone, without a friend in the world; for her father noticed nothing of what was taking place.

The time came when her father, the merchant, had to travel to distant parts in the course of his business. He bade farewell to his wife and kissed Vasilissa, giving her his blessing, and bade his step-daughters remember him while he was gone from home.

No sooner was he on his way than his wife sold the house, packed up all their belongings, and moved into a dwelling far from the village and on the outskirts of a deep and gloomy forest. Vasilissa was soon forced into the forest looking for rare herbs, flowers and berries while her stepsisters sat in comfort, warming themselves by the fire.

For Vasilissa's step-mother well knew there lived deep in the forest, in a rickety hut, an old Baba-Yaga, a witch grandmother, who ate people as other people eat chickens. This is just what the step-mother hoped would happen to Vasilissa. But always the girl returned home safe and sound, for did she not have her dead mother's doll to protect her and warn her away from danger? The merchant's wife grew to hate her even more.

One autumn evening the woman set each of the three girls a task. Her eldest daughter was to make a square of lace, her younger was to knit a pair of stockings and Vasilissa was to spin a basket of flax. The wife gave the three maidens instructions, then put out all of the fires in the house, leaving only a single candle burning in the room where the girls were working. Then she went to bed and slept.

For three hours the girls worked away at their tasks until the elder daughter took up the tongs to trim the candle, but, as her mother had bidden her, she stumbled and snuffed out the candle, as though by accident.

"What shall we do now?" asked her sister. "The fires are out, there is no light in the house and our tasks are still unfinished."

"One of us must go to the forest to fetch a light from the fire of the old Baba-Yaga," said the first.

Both girls rounded on Vasilissa and drove her out into the night. They bade her not return without fire, or it would be the worse for her.

Vasilissa had put a shawl around her shoulders before stepping out into the night. From one pocket she now took her doll, and from the other she drew the supper she had already prepared for it. Sitting down by an old fir tree she said, "There, my little doll. Always you have come to my aid and advised me well. Tell me, what should I do now?"

As always, the doll's eyes lit up. In the darkness of the night they twinkled like stars. After she had eaten a little and drunk a little she said, "Have no fear, Vasilissa, all will be well. Go where you are sent and have no fear of the witch. You will come to no harm." So Vasilissa put the doll back into her pocket and began to make her way into the dark and gloom of the forest.

On and on she trudged, until at last she heard the sound of horse's hoofs and a man on horseback galloped past her, just as the dawn was beginning to break. In the pale light she could see that he was dressed completely in white; the horse he rode was as white as milk, and its harness shone like snow.

A little further on she heard the sound of more galloping, and another horseman galloped past her. He was dressed completely in red; the horse he rode was blood-red and its harness shone crimson in the sun, which rose at the moment of his passing.

All day the girl searched for the Baba-Yaga. Just before nightfall she came to the witch's rickety hut, made of human bones and standing on its hens' legs. On its top were the skulls of humans. The gate in the wall had human bones for hinges and the locks were jaw-bones set with sharp teeth. Fear turned Vasilissa to stone and she stood as still as a post rooted in the ground.

Even as she stared wide-eyed, a third rider came galloping by. His face was jet black, he was clad in black and his horse shone like wet coal. He galloped to the gate of the hut, then disappeared from sight as though he had sunk through the ground. Even as he did so the night fell, and the forest became dark and still.

At the same moment the eyes of all the skulls on the walls of the hut lit up until the area was as bright as day. Vasilissa was now shaking with fear, but her feet refused to move and she stood still, as though nailed to the spot.

Suddenly the wood was swept with a fearful noise. Trees groaned and swayed as the Baba-Yaga came flying through the forest. Her chariot was a giant iron mortar, or mixing pot, which she drove with a pestle. As she flew she swept away the trail she left behind her with a kitchen broom. Right up to the gate of the house she rode, then stopped, and began to sing:

Little House, little House,
Stand the way your mother placed thee,
Turn your back on the forest, and face me!

Right away the little house turned to face the witch, then stood still. Sniffing all around her, the old Baba-Yaga cried, "Fee, fi, fo, fum; I smell the blood of a Russian! Who is here?"

Vasilissa was very frightened, but she stepped forward to the old woman and said, "It is Vasilissa, old grandmother. I have been sent to you by my step-sisters to fetch a light for their candle."

"Well, well," said the Baba-Yaga. "I know them both, and I'll give you fire. But in return you must work to pay for it. Otherwise I shall eat you for supper." Then she turned to the gate of the house and called, "You, my bony locks, unlock! You, my stout gate, open up!" Immediately the gate unlocked of its own accord and flew wide open. The Baba-Yaga strode inside, whistling. Vasilissa followed close behind her, and as soon as she passed across the threshold the gate swung shut and the lock snapped tight.

No sooner had Vasilissa entered the hut than the witch settled herself down by the fire, stretched out her long, bony legs and said, "Go to the oven and fetch my supper and lay it on the table."

Vasilissa did as she was bid. To her amazement there was enough meat in the oven to feed at least three strong men. Then the witch bade the girl fetch a barrel of beer from the cellar. The old woman fell to and ate and drank heartily, leaving only a portion of cabbage soup, a crust of bread and a morsel of meat for the girl.

Once her hunger was satisfied the Baba-Yaga lay down drowsily by the stove and said; "Listen well, and do what I tell you. In the morning, when I've gone, clean up the yard, sweep out the house and prepare my supper. Then take a measure of wheat from my storehouse and pick out all the black grains and wild peas. Do everything that I tell you; otherwise I'll have you for my supper."

As soon as the old woman was asleep Vasilissa took her doll out of her pocket and set out its supper. As always the doll's eyes lit up. She ate a little and drank a little, then said, "Don't despair, Vasilissa the Beautiful. Be calm and sleep. Tomorrow will be wiser than today." Vasilissa was content.

When Vasilissa awoke it was still dark. She rose and looked out the window.

The lights in the skulls on the wall were still burning. As she was looking, the man dressed in white, riding his milk-white steed, galloped round the corner of the hut and disappeared. Just then the dawn broke, and the lights in the skulls went out. The old witch was in the yard. When she whistled the mortar and pestle and kitchen broom flew to her side. While she was climbing into the mortar the man dressed in red, mounted on his blood-red horse, galloped like the wind around the corner of the hut just as the sun rose above the trees.

The Baba-Yaga's locks unfastened at her command, the gate flew open and she rode off in her mortar, driving with the pestle and sweeping away her trail with the broom.

Vasilissa prepared to do all that the Baba-Yaga had commanded, but to her joy she discovered that the yard was already cleaned, the floors swept and her little doll was in the granary picking the last of the black specks and wild peas out of a measure of wheat.

Hugging her little doll, Vasilissa cried, "You wonderful doll. Now I have only to cook the Baba-Yaga's supper. You've done everything else for me!"

"Cook it, Vasilissa, and may the cooking of it make you healthy." So spoke the doll; then the twinkle went out of its eyes, and it became a doll again.

So Vasilissa spent the day resting and gathering her strength. Towards evening she laid the table and prepared a fine supper, and looked out of the window watching for the return of the witch. As she did so she heard the sound of galloping hoofs, and the jet-black man on the coal-black steed galloped up to the gate in the wall and disappeared, even as the sun set and the eyes of the skulls lit up as the flames were kindled.

Once again the Baba-Yaga's return was heralded by the groaning of trees and a whirlwind of scattered leaves.

"Well, have you done all that I asked you?" She cackled, and went poking about this way and that until she was satisfied that Vasilissa had left no task undone. She was not too well pleased to find that all was in order, but after a fine supper with a goodly measure of beer she prepared to sleep. But not before she had clapped her hands and shouted, "Ho! Ho! my faithful servants! My true friends! Haste and grind my wheat!" No sooner had she spoken than three pairs of hands appeared, seized the measure of wheat and carried it away.

Then she commanded Vasilissa to do on the morrow what she had done that day, but in addition she was to take from the storehouse a measure of poppy-seeds and clean them one by one until they shone. Then she turned to the wall, and was soon snoring like a pig hunting for truffles.

As soon as she heard the old witch's snores Vasilissa again took out and fed her doll. Again the doll told her to do as the old crone bade her, and all would be well.

The next morning Vasilissa looked out once again, as the Baba-Yaga was riding away in her mortar. As the old crone disappeared, the man dressed in red,

126

riding his blood-red steed, galloped by at the very moment the sun rose over the forest.

As it happened the day before, so it happened again. The little doll completed Vasilissa's tasks for her and the girl was awaiting when the old witch returned. As had happened the day before, the man in black on the coal-black horse galloped up to the gate as darkness fell and the lights in the skulls glimmered and shone.

Again, the Baba-Yaga examined the house and the yard carefully, ate her supper, then clapped her hands and called, "Ho! Ho! my faithful servants! My true friends! Haste and press out the oil from my poppy-seeds." Once more three pairs of hands appeared and did as the hag commanded. Then, turning to Vasilissa, she said, "Well girl, aren't you going to say anything? Why just stand there dumb?"

"I didn't dare speak, old woman," replied the girl, "But with your permission I would like to ask you some questions."

"Ask away then," said the old witch, "but remember that not every question leads to a good answer. Beside, if you know too much, you will grow old too soon. Now what do you have to ask?"

"Tell me about the men on horseback," said Vasilissa. "As I was searching for your hut a man in white rode by on a milk-white steed. Who was he?"

"He was my servant — my white, bright day. He will do you no harm. Ask some more of me."

"Afterwards, a second rider galloped by. He was dressed in red and rode a blood-red steed. Who was he?"

"Another servant — the round, red sun. He will do you no harm. Ask some more of me."

"Then a third rider passed by; he was jet-black and rode a coal-black steed. Who was he?"

"Another servant — the dark, black night. He will do you no harm. Ask some more of me."

But Vasilissa, remembering that the Baba-Yaga had said that not every question leads to a good answer, was silent.

"Ask some more of me! Go on, ask some more of me!" the old witch snorted. "Why don't you ask about the three hands that carry out my orders?"

Vasilissa saw that the witch was growing angry so answered her gently. "Three questions are enough for me. As you said, old lady, if I know too much I'll be old too soon."

"As well for you, too," snarled the witch. "For had you asked about those hands they would have seized you, too, and done to you what they did to my wheat and my poppy-seeds. Very well, then. But, tell me, how did you do all the tasks I set for you each day?"

127

Vasilissa grew frightened as she saw the old witch's mounting anger so didn't dare tell her about her doll. Instead she said, "It is the blessing of my dead mother which helps me."

In a fury the Baba-Yaga leapt to her feet. "Be gone this instant," she shouted. "I'll have no blessings in this house. Away with you. At once!"

Vasilissa ran out from the house and as she did the witch shouted at the locks of the gate, which opened wide to allow the girl to pass through. Then the Baba-Yaga seized one of the skulls with its burning eyes and flung it after the girl. "There," she screamed, "is the fire for your step-sisters' candle. Take it and go. That is what you came for. Now be gone!"

Vasilissa quickly snatched up the skull, which she placed on the end of a stick and used as a torch to find her way through the forest to her step-mother's house. As she drew near to the gate she flung the skull into the bushes, thinking, "Surely, by now they will have found some fire." But the skull called out to her, "Pick me up, Vasilissa the Beautiful, and take me in to your step-mother." When she looked through the window, Vasilissa could see no glimmer of light at all, so she picked up the skull and carried it into the house with her.

Now while Vasilissa had been away, the step-mother and her two daughters had had no fire or light at all in the house. If they struck a flint with steel the tinder would not catch. If they borrowed fire from their neighbours it would go out immediately they took it inside the house. So they had no fire to cook over or with which to warm themselves. The nights were long and fearsome.

So when Vasilissa arrived with the light, they for once welcomed her in. When they set the skull up by the hearth and it remained burning they were delighted, and began to crow with pleasure.

Suddenly the eyes of the skull began to glow with the intensity of hot coals, and wherever Vasilissa's step-mother and her daughters moved the eyes followed them. They grew brighter and brighter, until they were like two furnaces. Then they became a consuming fire, so hot that the merchant's wicked wife and her two daughters burst into flames and were burned to ashes. But Vasilissa the Beautiful was unharmed.

When morning came Vasilissa dug a deep hole in the forest and buried the skull. Then she locked up the house and walked to the village, where she begged an old lady to give her shelter until her father should return from his journey.

Days passed and still her father did not appear. So Vasilissa begged some flax from the old woman in order to spin, and so pass away the weary days of waiting. As she spun, the thread came away from the spindle as fine as a lady's hair, and as bright. Soon there was enough thread to begin weaving. But the old lady had no loom, and the girl could find no one in the village to make one for her.

As she had learned to do at such times, Vasilissa went into her closet and took her doll from her pocket. After the doll had eaten a little and drunk a little, its

128

eyes began to shine and it said, "Fetch me an old frame and a basket of hair from a horse's mane, and I will arrange everything as you desire." Vasilissa did as the doll told her, went to bed, and the next morning, why, there was a loom, perfectly made, ready for the weaving to begin.

So Vasilissa began to weave; week after week, month after month, the whole winter through, until there emerged from the loom a length of linen so fine that it could well have passed through the eye of a needle.

When spring came, Vasilissa bleached the linen to the colour of freshly-fallen snow, which shone like polar ice. Then she said to the old woman. "Take this linen to the market place and perhaps what you get for it will pay for my food and lodging." But when the old woman saw such fine and dazzling linen, she said, "Never could I sell cloth like this in the market place. It is fit to be worn by no one but the tzar himself. Tomorrow I shall take it to the palace."

So the very next day the old woman went to the tzar's splendid palace and walked up and down before the windows. When the servants enquired as to her errand she replied not a word, but continued to walk back and forth. At last the tzar himself opened a window and called out, "What do you want, old woman? Why do you walk back and forth without saying a thing?"

"O majestic tzar!" the old woman replied, "I have here, in my basket, a length of linen cloth so wonderful that it is fit only for the eyes of your Majesty! I will show it to no one but you."

The tzar bade the old woman bring the cloth into the palace, and when he saw its beauty and fineness he was determined to have it for himself. "How much do you want for it, old woman?" he asked.

"There is no price for such a cloth, your Majesty. I have brought it to you for a gift. Please take it."

The tzar was amazed and delighted. He couldn't thank the old woman enough. He accepted the linen cloth, but sent the old woman home, laden with gifts.

Seamstresses were hired to make from the cloth shirts for the tzar. But when it had been cut up, the texture was so fine that there was not one of them he would trust to sew it. The best seamstresses in the kingdom were summoned, but not one dared undertake the task of sewing the tzar's shirts. At last the tzar sent for the old woman and said, "If you were able to spin such fine thread and weave such linen from it, then surely you must be able to sew shirts fit for a tzar."

"O tzar's majesty," replied the old woman, "it was not I who wove the linen, it was the work of my adopted daughter."

"Take it to her, then," commanded the tzar, "and tell her that I wish her to sew shirts for me that will do justice to the quality of the cloth."

The old woman took home the cloth and told Vasilissa of the tzar's wish. "Indeed, I knew that the sewing would have to be done by my own hands," said Vasilissa.

So locking herself into her own chamber, she began to sew the shirts. She worked so quickly that soon a dozen of the finest shirts ever seen were ready to be taken to the tzar. The old woman took them off to the palace while Vasilissa washed her face, did up her hair, and sat down by the window dressed in her finest gown.

Presently a servant in the tzar's livery arrived from the palace and came to the house. He entered and said, "The tzar, our lord, desires to meet for himself the clever needlewoman who has created such fine shirts, and to reward her with his own hands."

Vasilissa gathered herself together and accompanied the servant to the palace. As soon as the tzar saw her his heart swelled with love. He took her by the hand and bade her sit beside him. "Vasilissa the Beautiful," he said, "if you will but be my wife, I promise that never shall we be parted, as long as we both shall live."

So Vasilissa the Beautiful and the tzar were wed. And when the bride's father returned from his journey to far places, he and the old woman lived in splendour and comfort at the palace, in joy and utter contentment. Vasilissa lived on to a peaceful old age, but always in her pocket she carried her beloved dolly, given to her by her mother on her death-bed.

Pocahontas

Pocahontas was born, probably in 1596, at Werowocomoco, the principal residence of her father Powhatan, an American Indian chief. Powhatan ruled a loose alliance of Algonkion Indians in Virginia. In 1607 English colonists led by Captain John Smith founded the settlement of Jamestown on Indian territory. Relations between the white settlers and the Indians were uneasy, but it is said that the young Pocahontas, whose name meant "playful one", appeared not infrequently in the streets of Jamestown, becoming well known to many of the white citizens. She even seems to have acted as an emissary between her father and the colonists.

In December 1607, Captain John Smith, while on a trading expedition into Indian territory, was attacked and taken captive. The leader of the Indian party, Opechananough, said that Smith was to be taken to Powhatan. He was led through the forest for nearly two hours and then placed in a hut under guard for the night.

At that time of the year it was bitterly cold, and Smith was grateful for the return of his cloak the next morning. For now he was taken on a march lasting about five days, until at last he was led to Powhatan's "palace", the largest native building the captain had yet seen in Virginia. Inside awaited the bedecked chief. Beside him sat his favourite daughter, Pocahontas.

Later Captain Smith wrote that when the party arrived at Werowocomoco he was taken to the residence of the Indian "emperor" who was "proudly lying upon a bedstead a foot high, upon ten or twelve mats, richly hung with many chains of great pearls about his neck, and covered with great coverings of raccoon skins. At his head sat one woman, at his feet another. On each side, sitting upon a mat on the ground, were ranged his chief men on each side of the fire, ten in a rank, and behind them as many young women, each with a great

131

chain of white beads over their shoulders, their heads painted in red. And Powhatan with such a grave and majestic countenance as drove me into admiration to see such a state in a naked savage."

As the captain was ushered into Powhatan's presence, the assembled company gave a mighty shout. Then one of the chieftains brought water to the captive, so that he could wash his hands, and a bunch of feathers to use as a towel. Platters of food were placed before him and he was invited to eat.

While Smith was eating, it was obvious that the Indians were deciding what to do with him. Smith writes: "They then held a great consultation about me, and the conclusion was that I was to die, a fate which, in truth, was near coming to pass, but for God's goodness, as you shall hear. And indeed, it did seem as if my last hour was at hand, for as many of the savages as could laid hold of me, and having brought two great stones, which they placed before Powhatan, they dragged me to them, and laid my head thereon, making ready with their clubs to beat out my brains.

"But now, mark the mercy of God towards me when in this evil case, for surely it was his handiwork. Their clubs were raised, and in another moment I should have been dead, when Pocahontas, the King's dearest daughter, a child of ten years old, finding no entreaties could prevail to save me, darted forward, and, taking my head in her arms, laid her own upon it, and thus prevented my death. She thus claimed me as her own, and for her sake Powhatan was contented that I should live."

As his captors released their prisoner, the young Indian girl pulled him to his feet. Captain John Smith and Pocahontas were face to face for the first time.

It was then that Powhatan's grim visage relaxed a little, and slowly it became clear to the Englishman that not only was his life no longer in danger, but that he was free to return to Jamestown.

Although Smith had not understood at the time what was happening, it would now seem certain that he was being used in a ceremony, a ritual in which he was undergoing a mock execution before being accepted into Powhatan's tribe. John Smith was not to know that, and for the remainder of his days he would tell the story of the brave Indian girl, Pocahontas, who saved his life.

But for Pocahontas, her contact with the white settlers was to bring tremendous changes to her life.

In the spring of that year she became a frequent visitor to the fort at Jamestown, turning cartwheels, performing handsprings, and frolicking like the young girl she was. She and John Smith became good friends. He was fascinated by her youth and vitality and found her a welcome contrast to the grumbling settlers with whom he was living cheek by jowl. He would trade with the girl, giving her bits of copper and nick-nacks in exchange for Indian beads and baskets. The girl, in turn, liked the white man; he was good-humoured and well-mannered. The two respected each other. Besides, had not her father adopted the white man into the tribe, so that he was her countryman, her brother? They had a special relationship.

Pocahontas was also teaching John Smith something of her own language, and from him and the young boys of the settlement, whom she challenged in contests of leaping and running, she learnt to speak in English. One of her favourite phrases, taught to her by the boys, was "Love you not me?" which she was fond of repeating over and over, like a small, bright parrot.

But although John Smith and Pocahontas remained good friends, not all the other settlers and officials treated the Indians fairly. Too often they tried to take advantage of them in their trading. Powhatan was too astute not to know what was happening. He and his braves wanted guns and cannons — "thunder balls" — from the whites, who only offered them beads and trinkets in exchange for the Indian corn, which they needed desperately for food. So the Indians stole what they thought they deserved, and in retaliation John Smith took seven of their men captive, and held them prisoner in Jamestown.

It was then that Pocahontas accepted a new role. It was she, a proud princess, the daughter of the mighty Powhatan who went to Jamestown not to beg or plead, but to carry gifts and make it clear that her father expected the release of his men. Smith's affection and respect for Pocahontas won the day, and he released the captives into her custody. First, however, they must attend a church service, for John Smith was determined that the Indians should worship his god, whether they understood his ways or not.

From that time onward Powhatan's suspicions of the settlers increased, and there was continued trouble between the two races.

When John Smith was elected president of the settlement at Jamestown in September 1608 he was ordered by the London Company who were trading in the area to have Powhatan crowned as a subsidiary king to King James of England. So John Smith set out once again for Werowocomoco to invite Powhatan to Jamestown for the coronation.

It was Pocahontas who ceremoniously welcomed John Smith. The sacred fire was lit and Pocahontas herself, her body painted and wearing horns as a helmet, led a troupe of Indian girls in a wild dance. With shrill but lusty shouts and whoops they brandished their weapons as they danced to the sun and to John Smith's God, and made Smith welcome. "Love you not me?" she called, knowing little of what she was saying.

Powhatan was reluctant to be crowned by the colonists, and deep in his heart he saw the ceremony for the sham it was. He refused to kneel, but bent his head slightly and only long enough to receive the copper crown sent from England.

Instead of the Indians and the settlers drawing closer together, hostility increased on both sides. When she heard of a plot to murder John Smith, it was

Pocahontas who hurried through the forest at night to warn him and bid him flee before it was too late. She even warned him against taking food from her people lest it be poisoned. This time the Indian girl did indeed save the life of the white man whom she regarded as her brother. They were not to meet again for almost eight years.

But Pocahontas couldn't save John Smith from the enmity of his own people. A new governor appointed by the king was coming from England. Not only was John Smith to be relieved of his presidency, but there was a further plot among the settlers to assassinate him. It was with relief that Smith sailed for London to escape for a while the tensions of the colony.

When Sir Thomas Dale was made the acting governor of the colony in 1611, he was determined to rule the Indian population by force, if necessary. So Powhatan withdrew further inland, away from the areas of white settlement.

Pocahontas was now about seventeen years old. She had married an Indian called Kocoum, but the marriage must have been short-lived. In April of 1613 she was living at the home of a Potomac chief when Captain Samuel Argall arrived in the district from Jamestown to trade with the Indians.

In the course of his exchanges Argall learnt from some Indians that Pocahontas was in the district, and he saw at once a clever way of dealing with Powhatan. If he could kidnap the old chief's favourite daughter he would have a weapon stronger than cannons.

So he arranged an invitation for Pocahontas to visit his ship. His old friend, Iapassus, brother of the Potomac chief, would do anything for a copper kettle. The wife of Iapassus, a loud-mouthed woman, was even more covetous of the white man's goods. So it was one of her own people who lured Pocahontas on board Argall's ship. Perhaps she was anxious to renew her friendship with the colonists. Certainly Argall received her courteously and kindly. He even offered her a couch on which to rest awhile. But Pocahontas was anxious, and entreated Iapassus and his wife to take her ashore. It was when they left her behind, refusing to take her with them, that Pocahontas realised that she was a prisoner, even though Argall assured her that she was his noble guest and that she would be honoured as a princess.

Unbeknown to Pocahontas, Argall dispatched messengers to Powhatan, promising to restore his daughter in exchange for the Englishmen whom he held prisoner and a handsome booty, but in actual fact he sailed back to Jamestown, with Pocahontas as his enforced guest.

So Pocahontas was seen once more in Jamestown. Although she had actually been kidnapped by Argall, she was treated as an Indian princess and was taken into the care of Alexander Whitaker, a missionary clergyman who had a hundred-acre parsonage upriver at Rock Hall. At the request of Sir Thomas Dale, Whitaker began to instruct Pocahontas in the Christian faith. She was dressed in the fashion of the day and her feet squeezed into tight leather-soled shoes.

Powhatan sent messages to say he could not meet the demands of the white men. To Pocahontas it seemed that she had been deserted by her own father. But she was made of fine fibre; she would not be cowed. Rather, she would play out her role as a member of a royal family, but in a white society.

It was then that she met at church a handsome, 28-year-old widower called John Rolfe, who was growing tobacco in Virginia from seeds he had come by in Trinidad, to sell in England. Soon John Rolfe was a frequent visitor at the parsonage and was much in the company of Pocahontas. As he helped her with her English he became more and more enamoured of the playful girl who now adopted the part of a princess. She felt a return of the affection she had had for John Smith but now it was more than affection; it was love.

It was not easy for the sternly religious John Rolfe to contemplate marriage with an Indian girl, even if she were of royal birth. But now that Pocahontas was a Christian, he believed that it was God's will that he marry her. Sir Thomas Dale and other British officials thought it was a splendid idea. It would secure a treaty between the two races.

When Pocahontas's brothers visited her to see how the English were treating her, she assured them that she knew what she was doing. Powhatan hadn't been willing to fight for her, or to respond to Argall's demands, so she would go ahead and marry Rolfe.

This she did on 5 April 1614, in the church at Jamestown. Powhatan, who had refused ever again to visit an English settlement, sent an old uncle of Pocahontas, called Opachisco, to represent him at the ceremony, and two of his sons to be witnesses.

Sir Thomas Dale, the governor, was delighted, and it appeared that peace had at last come to the opposing races. A treaty was drawn up, and both sides seemed happy. The "Peace of Pocahontas" had turned the Indians into friends.

News of the marriage was hailed with delight in London as was that of the birth of a son, Thomas, a year later. Politicians and churchmen alike congratulated themselves on the happiness caused by this union of two races.

It was not surprising then, that in 1616 when Sir Thomas Dale was returning to London he should take Pocahontas, her husband and her baby along with him.

The party travelled in style, with about a dozen Indian attendants and Matachanna, a sister to Pocahontas, to help look after baby Thomas. An ambassador of Powhatan, Tomocomo, also accompanied the party. He was to report to Powhatan what life in England was really like, and to find out what had happened to Captain John Smith.

Pocahontas's life was now dramatically different to that of her wild, carefree youth. Gone were the days of half-naked handsprings and cartwheels. No longer could she track her way through forest glades, creeping up on the raccoons as they scratched and raked, or spying on beavers building their dams across the gurgling streams.

Instead she rustled along in stiff petticoats and voluminous garments that chafed and irritated her. The sound of wind in the leaves and echoing bird calls were replaced by the clang of church bells, the cries of hawkers and the constant clatter of carriages making their way through the crowded, cobbled streets.

The dark, grey air of London choked the girl from Virginia, who loved wide blue skies that at night glittered with the light from countless stars.

And where was her friend John Smith? Pocahontas knew that he was in London. Indeed, she knew that he had written to Queen Anne of Great Britain about her, telling her majesty how "this Lady Pocahontas" had "hazarded the beating out of her brains to save mine". He had even gone on to relate how she, Pocahontas, had been tricked into captivity and how she had created peace between her people and the English, "and at last rejecting her barbarous condition, was married to an English gentleman, with whom at this present she is in England; the first Christian ever of that Nation, the first Virginian ever spake English, or had a child in marriage by an Englishman: a matter surely, if my meaning be truly considered and well understood, worthy of a Prince's understanding."

So Pocahontas and her husband were invited to the court masque on Twelfth Night, in 1617. She was used to people staring at her in the streets, then turning aside to talk about her. At the masque she was the centre of attention. But well she knew her position. She was Powhatan's daughter and proud of her lineage.

The Virginia Company had allotted her a small stipend of £4 a week for the maintenance of herself and Thomas. The Rolfe family lived for a time early in their London sojourn at an inn just outside Ludgate, called the Belle Sauvage. Although the inn had borne that name for over one hundred years, Pocahontas made it famous. The owner even had a sign painted with Pocahontas on it. At the Belle Sauvage, Pocahontas met literary figures such as the "rare" Ben Johnson, who was to include mention of her in his plays.

Probably John Rolfe took his wife and child to Norfolk on a visit to his mother, for there was later, at Heacham Hall where she then lived, a mulberry tree, popularly called "Pocahontas's mulberry tree".

Pocahontas was also entertained by dignitaries such as the Bishop of London, who, according to the Reverend Samuel Purchas, "entertained her with festive state and pomp beyond what I have seen in his great hospitality to other ladies". Of Pocahontas, Purchas wrote that she "carried herself as the daughter of a King".

But where was John Smith? Pocahontas longed to see him again.

The stinking lanes around Ludgate did nothing for Pocahontas's health, already in a weakened state from her new lifestyle. So the Rolfes moved to Brentford, to the west of London, where there was a river and remnants of ancient forests. It was a more fitting and tranquil abode for the Indian Princess. John Smith, who may have been overawed by the treatment being given to Pocahontas, still didn't contact her or visit her. Was she not a protégé of Lady De La Warne who had taken her in hand? Had she not sat with royalty at the Court's Christmas festival? Perhaps John Smith felt that he would be an intrusion into the life of this fêted person.

Whatever delayed his visit, John Smith, in the autumn of 1616, could no longer stay away. He was preparing to sail for New England. Before he left England he must call on Pocahontas.

When, at last, the old friends met, Pocahontas seemed not able to cope. Smith was to say in a letter to a friend, "After a modest salutation, without any word, she turned about, (and) obscured her face, as not seeming well contented." John Smith and the party withdrew, and Pocahontas was left alone with her emotions.

Who would know what battles were being waged in the heart of the playful girl of the woods, now a gowned lady and a celebrity? Her kinsman, Tomocomo, had no time for the Englishman's king or his god. He preferred to dress in Indian fashion and still painted and feathered himself even when arguing about religion with the Bishop of London. But what did Pocahontas really believe?

After Pocahontas had recovered her equanimity John Smith returned, and she addressed him at length. She reminded him of their happy friendship in days gone by in Virginia; of all that she had done for him and his people. She reminded Smith, too, that he had called Powhatan "father" in a strange land, "and by the same reason, so must I do you". When John Smith demurred, she broke in with some impatience, "Were you not afraid to come into my father's country? Did you not cause fear in him, and all his people (but me)? And fear you that I should call you father? I tell you then, I will, and you shall call me child, so I will be for ever and ever your countryman." She had believed him dead until she arrived in Plymouth. Why had he taken so long to come and greet her?

John Smith had little to say in return. He departed, and Pocahontas never saw him again.

Now her husband was anxious to get back to his tobacco fields. He had been made secretary of the colony of Virginia, and was eager to return to Jamestown. Pocahontas did not want to go. She begged Rolfe to let them all stay. Would she be able to resume a life back in Virginia where her husband would be forever seeking to convert her people from their ancient ways and beliefs? Perhaps he would expect her to help him in his campaign against the lifestyle of what he called "poore, wretched and mysbelieving people". Could she do that?

And her physical strength was being sapped by the damp winds of winter. She coughed incessantly, and felt always tired. Two of her Indian household died from the bleak climate that winter. Apart from what would await her in Virginia, Pocahontas would have to face a long, trying voyage home.

But Rolfe insisted. He was her husband. It was her Christian duty to bow to his will.

So even though Pocahontas was ill in body and spirit, she and what was left of her Indian household embarked on the ship *George*, bound for Virginia and commanded by now Admiral Samuel Argall, in March 1617. Tomocomo was delighted. He wanted only to leave the distaste he felt for London well behind him. Pocahontas didn't; something of that strange environment had entered her soul.

On board the *George*, Pocahontas was taken to her sleeping quarters. She was too ill to stand at the rail as the ship was guided slowly downstream along the Thames towards Gravesend, twenty-five miles from London. It was a depressing, funereal voyage. Pocahontas lay coughing, desperately ill.

It seems ironic that the *George* should drop anchor at a place called Gravesend. Pocahontas begged to be taken ashore. In a bustling inn not far from the wharf Pocahontas was hurried to a room, knowing that her end was near. "All men must die," she told her husband. She died, "having given great demonstration of her Christian sincerity, as the first fruits of Virginian conversion, leaving her a goodly memory, and the hopes of her resurrection." So wrote the Reverend Samuel Purchas.

Who knows what was in her heart? Perhaps she was reaching out to the great sun and to her god, who were waiting to welcome her.

Pocahontas was buried at the Parish Church of St. George, Gravesend, where the inaccuracy of the inscription underscores the tragedy of her life:

"1616 (1617) (March) 21 Rebecca Wrolfe wyffe of Thomas Wrolf gent. A Virginia lady borne, was buried in the chauncell."

The Rolfe's infant son, Thomas, was not well, and he was landed at Plymouth. He was left in the care of his uncle, Henry Rolfe, and did not visit Virginia until he was twenty years old and confirmed in English ways.

Mary Bryant

On 21 July 1792 the *Dublin Chronicle* printed a report from the Public Office, Bow Street, London, headed "Wonderful Escape from Botany Bay", which begins: "On Saturday, the 7th July, James Martin, John Butcher, William Allen, Nathaniel Lilley and Mary Bryant were brought by several of Sir Sampson Wright's officers, from on board the *Gorgon* frigate, to this office. They are all that survive of eleven persons who escaped from the settlement at Sydney Cove."

Mary Bryant's story begins in Exeter two years before the arrival of the First Fleet. She was then Mary Broad.

When Mary Broad stood before the judge at the Exeter assizes she was a young woman of about twenty-two years of age. She had been born at Fowey, a small port in Cornwall, and grew up when times were hard and work was scarce. Early in her life she learned to fend for herself. "The Lord helps them what help themselves," she told herself grimly the day that she was charged with assault and robbery. She had taken the lady's cloak, because it was perishing with cold and surely the likes of her had plenty more. As for the assault — well, she really hadn't hurt the woman badly, let alone killed her. But deep down she was uneasy. The penalty in those grim days for assault and robbery was death, and Mary Broad knew of plenty who had ended their days on the gallows for even less than that.

Fate was on the side of Mary Broad that day — or was it the proud, almost defiant look in her eye? Did the judge recognise something of the spirit that had seen a country girl survive thus far, and would see her through worse ordeals than she could have dreamed of that day in Exeter? Or was it just pity for her sex? Well, Mary Broad didn't give a fig for that. "I'm as good as any man, and better than most," she said to herself when the judge passed sentence. No, it wasn't to be death after all. "Pardon," Mary called it, "seven years at Botany Bay!" Why, Mary Broad didn't even know where it was, hadn't even heard of it. But, the time was coming when it would be a harsh reality, a memory never to be erased.

Mary Broad's life had been, and always would be, governed by strange, capricious circumstances. It was in the year of her trial that Britain's Prime Minister, William Pitt, made the decision to found a settlement at Botany Bay. A penal colony peopled by convicts, it was to be, and women would be necessary to help turn a prison camp into a settlement.

So Mary Broad spent weary months in prison waiting for the ships of the fleet to be made ready. By the time she was herded onto the convict ship, *Charlotte*, she was already pregnant to a fellow prisoner, although some say she was raped by a gaoler. Mary was never one to allow the grass to grow under her feet. If there was ever any opportunity to soften the harshness of her life, she would snatch it. Life in prison, and even on a convict ship, was a little more tolerable with a companion.

It was early on Sunday morning, 13 Mary 1787, when Mary set sail for her new life on the other side of the world. Before she arrived at Botany Bay, Mary gave birth to her daughter, whom she called Charlotte, after the ship on which she sailed. On 10 February 1788, soon after landing in the new colony, Mary married William Bryant, a Cornish fisherman. William, too, had been sentenced for seven years, for smuggling and resisting revenue officers. "Would they ever see England again?", they wondered. Mary was certain in her mind that they would, and maybe before seven years were up. Who knew? Life was full of opportunities. All one had to do was grasp one when it came along.

Mary and William didn't have to wait long, although it seemed long enough. Food was scarce and life was intolerably difficult. All around them men and women gave up hope of ever returning to their native country. Some even went about saying that they would all starve, for certain, if they didn't die from the heat or illness. Or else they would be murdered by the natives. But Mary never gave up hope. Life for her was for living. So she had another child, a son, whom she called Emmanuel, which means, "God is with us".

"I hope he is," thought Mary, "but even if he isn't I'll do what I can myself. This one will have a better life than I've had, if I have any say in it."

It was about the time that Emmanuel was born that William Bryant was put in charge of the boats that caught the fish for the settlement. His skill as a fisherman now paid off. Not only did he have a good, clean job out in the sunshine a lot of the time, but the family had food — and there was always the chance of a little trading on the side, — Mary saw to that — even though it once cost William one hundred lashes when he was caught selling fish that should have gone to the Government Store. And she saw to it that William kept his wits about him. Who knew? With a boat at his disposal, escape might just be possible. "Nothing ventured, nothing gained," Mary used to say. Just let the opportunity come!

Opportunity did come when an East Indies trader, the *Waaksambeyd*, under the command of a Captain Smit, sailed into Port Jackson from Batavia laden with stores and provisions for the colony. "Sweet talk, William," urged Mary. "You never know what you'll get until you try."

From his fishing expeditions William was well-known on the harbour, and he was a hail-fellow-well-met sort of person. Again, circumstances came to the aid of Mary Bryant, for, believe it or not, William was able to persuade the captain of the Dutch ship to sell him a chart, compass, quadrant, muskets and ammunition. Into the bargain, the captain gave him a hundred pounds of rice, and sold him fourteen pounds of pork, which the Bryants rolled in bark and hid under the floorboards of their hut. More sweet talk, and William was able to buy a hundred pounds of flour from the colony's baker. He was also able to set aside ten gallons of fresh water.

Mary could see freedom ahead; but she would have to plan well, and William would have to go carefully. They needed help. They couldn't escape alone. Carefully they approached seven other convicts they believed they could trust — John Butcher, James Martin, William Morton, Samuel Bird, James Cox, Nathaniel Lilley and William Allen. The seven didn't need much persuasion. Anything would be better than being marooned and starving at the end of the world. Who knew what could be in store for them?

Opportunity knocked once more, on the night of 28 March 1791. The *Waaksambeyd* had set sail and there were no other ships in the harbour. Under cover of darkness William Bryant and his fellow convicts seized the governor's cutter. With Mary and Charlotte and baby Emmanuel on board, they silently sailed through the heads at the dark of the moon and headed north, up the east coast of Australia towards New Guinea.

For sixty-nine days the little company made its way in an open six-oared boat up the coast and around Cape York, across the Arafura Sea to Koepang, in Timor. They made port on 5 June 1791, having bravely sailed 3254 nautical miles in ten weeks.

Although they arrived safely in Timor, there were times on the voyage when the men of the crew were grateful for Mary Bryant's determination to sail steadily forward, and her unfailing ability to remain cheerful, always firm in her belief that opportunity had to be firmly grasped whenever it offered itself.

For the first five weeks it rained constantly. There was little comfort to be had either at sea or when they put in to shore. Their provisions gave them only enough food for survival, and when it didn't rain they had to ration the water supply drastically.

When they were ashore they drew up a roster for keeping watch while the party slept; otherwise, they believed, they would have been massacred by the

natives, or their boat would have been stolen. On several occasions when it seemed that they were to be attacked, they discharged the two old muskets that Bryant had obtained from Captain Smit, firing over the heads of their attackers to frighten them off.

Somehow or other, James Martin was able to keep a journal, in which he recorded their progress. From his account it would seem that Mary Bryant and her fellow travellers were the first white people to sail into the Hunter River, to enter Port Stephens and Moreton Bay and to make anchorage within the Barrier Reef. They were the first to discover coal in Australia, north of Port Jackson, where later great coalfields were to be opened up.

It is clear from Martin's journal that the men were superb navigators, but even clearer is the courage and determination which drove them on. Mary Bryant with her three-year-old girl and her baby boy helped provide the party with backbone.

When the boat let in water they had to haul it ashore and treat it with beeswax and resin. Once they had to resort to putting soap in the seams. For three weeks they made their way along the coast looking for a suitable harbour or a creek so that they could land and search for fresh water. At last they chose a spot where the surf was relatively calm, and two of the convicts swam ashore, but they made their way back to the boat at once when they saw a crowd of hostile natives coming towards them.

Not long afterwards the surf became so strong and the boat began taking in so much water that to lighten it the escapees had to throw overboard all their excess clothing. Martin was to write: "That night we ran into an open bay, but could see no place to land as the surf was so strong that we were afraid of having our boat smashed to pieces. That night we anchored in the bay but our grappling broke and we were driven into the middle of the surf, expecting every moment that our boat would be battered to pieces and every soul would perish. But, as God would have it, we got our boat safe to shore without any loss or damage excepting one oar. We hauled our boat up and there remained two days and two nights.

There we kindled a fire with great difficulty. Everything that we had was very wet. We found plenty of shell fish, and there was fresh water. The natives came down in great numbers, but we discharged a musket over their heads and they dispersed immediately, so that we saw no more of them."

On another occasion when the party landed on a beach they saw two native women carrying fire sticks. The sailors made signs, no doubt assisted by Mary Bryant, who never allowed any chance to slip by, and they were able to kindle a fire and rest up for two days.

But when they set to sea again, they drove straight into a heavy gale and were quickly swept far out to sea by a strong current. All night the small boat was tossed about at the whim of the waves, which Martin says were "running mountains high". Then the rain fell in torrents, and the tiny crew had to bail continually to keep the boat afloat. At this point Martin records in his journal: "I will leave you to consider what a terrible condition and what distress the woman and the two little babies were in. Everything was so wet and there was no way that we could light a fire. We had nothing to eat but a little raw rice."

Far from complaining, Mary Bryant endured all the hardships and wretchedness in the belief that she, with her husband and her two children, was sailing to freedom and a better life.

By this time the party was well up towards Cape York. It was with great relief that they were able to find a passage through the reef surrounding one of the islands and pull into a little sandy beach. They hauled the boat up on to the shore, and after many attempts they were able to light a fire and cook a small quantity of rice. There was only one gallon of fresh water remaining, and not a drop could be found on the island. But they did find a host of turtles on the reef. They were able to turn five of them over and drag them up on to the beach. That night it rained, and they were able to catch water for all their needs. For six days they remained on the island and feasted on turtles and shell fish, which Martin records provided them with noble meals.

In the Gulf of Carpentaria they were attacked by natives in canoes, who fired "their bows and arrows at us," says Martin. By good fortune none of the arrows hit its mark, and the party was able to take a good look at the local inhabitants, including a chief who was heavily draped with strings of shells.

But although the sailors escaped the natives' arrows they were chased by over thirty warriors in a large canoe under mat-sail as they were making their way across the Gulf of Carpentaria. Again circumstance and good fortune came to their aid and their own sails filled with wind so that they were able to shake off their pursuers. They crossed the Gulf in five days. The party then headed straight for Timor and sailed into Koepang, on 5 June 1791.

When they told the Dutch governor there that they were survivors of a shipwreck they were well looked after. The governor fed and clothed them, and for two months the party worked happily for the Dutch settlers in Timor.

It was at this point that Mary Bryant's forthright tongue got her into trouble. This woman of action wasn't at all pleased to be spending time in Timor. She hadn't escaped from Port Jackson and endured ten weeks at sea for nothing. Not until she saw England again would she be content.

It was while she was upbraiding her drunken husband in no uncertain terms and in ringing tones for not being up and doing that she was overhead by one of the Dutch. When William Bryant was questioned he confessed that they were not shipwrecked sailors at all, but runaway convicts. The men and Mary were immediately imprisoned by the Dutch and cross-questioned by the Governor.

Although they were allowed out for a day, two at a time, the absconders were kept in prison until they were handed over to Captain Edwards, RN, who was to escort them to Batavia on board the *Rembang*, a ship belonging to the Dutch East India Company. The men were put in leg irons, called "the bilboes", until they reached Batavia.

There they were transferred, still in irons, to a Dutch guardship to await transportation back to England. The hardships of transportation, the severe conditions in the penal colony, along with the frightful ordeal of months at sea in an open boat with inadequate food proved too much for William Bryant. He was to die in Batavia of fever, as was Mary's baby son, Emmanuel. Perhaps William Bryant lacked the iron will and determination of the wife who survived him.

Six weeks later the convict party was broken up and put on three different ships bound for the Cape of Good Hope.

On the way to the Cape two of the men, Bird and Morton, died and Cox fell overboard and was drowned.

At the Cape the survivors, including Mary Bryant and Charlotte, were placed on board the *Gorgon* under the command of Captain Parker, bound for London.

The *Gorgon* was a man-of-war that was taking home marines from Botany Bay. They knew all about the daring escape of the convicts from Port Jackson, recognised the courage and endurance of Mary Bryant in particular, and, according to Martin, were glad that the convicts had not perished at sea.

Sadly, Mary's daughter did not survive the passage to England and died at sea on the fifth of May. Her mother and the remaining survivors arrived back in England in 1792, and were tried at the Old Bailey, convicted, and sent to Newgate prison to complete their sentences.

But by now Mary Bryant's grit and iron will was being recognised. Her strength of character and her determination to master unfortunate circumstance was gaining her the reputation of a heroine. The *Dublin Chronicle* report praised her in glowing terms: "The resolution displayed by this woman is hardly to be paralleled. At one time their anchor broke, and the surf was so great, that the men laid down their oars, in a state of despair, and gave themselves up as lost; but this amazon, taking one of their hats, cried out, 'Never fear!' and immediately began to exert herself in clearing the boat of water; her example was followed by her companions, and by great labour the boat was prevented from sinking, until they got into smoother sea."

The poor and oppressed saw in Mary Bryant hope that they could survive and even overcome their misfortunes. The rich and famous saw her as a battler, a woman to be admired. The famous writer and biographer, James Boswell, took up her cause and wrote letters to the Home Secretary and the Under Secretary of State, pleading for mercy and pardon on her behalf.

When she was released from prison in May 1793, Mary Bryant at last returned to her native Cornwall, now aged twenty-eight, but having experienced more than all the old women of her village put together. She had become a convict turned heroine. She was to receive from Boswell, "ten pounds yearly as long as she behaved well".

A letter dated November 1794, thanking Boswell for his help, is the last that history knows of Mary Bryant, but legend will ensure that she is remembered, if not in Cornwall, then at Botany Bay.

A packet of dried Australian "sweet tea" leaves, which Mary somehow miraculously held on to and which she gave to Boswell as a souvenir, is now kept in the archives of Yale University in America.

Bibliography

Ancient Greece
Cottrell, Arthur *A Dictionary of World Mythology,* Oxford University Press, 1990
Grimal, Pierre *Larousse World Mythology,* Hamlyn, 1977
Monaghan, Patricia *The Book of Goddesses and Heroines,* Llewellyn Publications, 1990
Pinsent, John *Greek Mythology,* Peter Bedrick Books, 1982
Stapleton, Michael *The Illustrated Dictionary of Greek and Roman Mythology,*
    Peter Bedrick Books, 1986

China
Christie, Anthony *Chinese Mythology,* Peter Bedrick Books, 1983
Sanders, Tao Tao Lie *Dragons, Gods and Spirits from Chinese Mythology,*
    Schocken Books, 1981

Jewish Champions
The Bible: Old Testament and Apocrypha; Joshua, Esther, Judith
Goldstein, David *Jewish Legends,* Peter Bedrick Books, 1987
Patterson, José *Angels, Prophets, Rabbis and Kings from the Stories of the Jewish People,*
    Peter Bedrick Books, 1991

Ancient Arabia
The Bible: Old Testament 1 Kings 10:1–10,13; 2 Chronicles 9: 1–9, 12
Ginzberg, Louis *The Legends of the Jews, Vol. iv,* Philadelphia: The Jewish Publication
    Society of America, 1913
The Thousand and One Nights trans. by N.J. Dawood, London: Penguin, 1954

A Warrior Queen
Matthews, John *Boadicea: Warrior Queen of the Celts,* Sterling, 1988

Saints and Holy Women
Farmer, David H. *The Oxford Dictionary of Saints,* 2nd ed., Oxford University Press, 1987
Sackville-West, Vita *Saint Joan of Arc,* Doubleday, 1991
Shaw, George Bernard *Saint Joan,* Penguin, 1946
Storr, Catherine *Joan of Arc,* Raintree, 1985

Against the Odds
Adams, Patricia *Pocahontas, Indian Princess,* Dell, 1987
Cushing, Frank H. *Zuni Folk Tales,* University of Arizona Press, 1986
Fritz, Jean *The Double Life of Pocahontas,* Putnam, 1987
Phelps, Ethel Johnston *The Maid of the North: Feminist Folktales from Around the World,*
    Holt, 1981
Riordan, James *The Woman in the Moon and other Tales of Forgotten Heroines,* Dial Books, 1985
Winthrop, Elizabeth *Vasilissa the Beautiful: A Russian Folktale,* HarperCollins
    Children's Books, 1991

Index